The Full Story of
ANDY MOOG

An Inspirational Story of a Hockey Icon Who Became a Pillar of Success and Stability in Net

Margaret Harris

Copyright © 2024 by Margaret Harris

All rights reserved. No part of this publication may be reproduced, distributed, or transmitted in any form or by any means, including photocopying, recording, or other electronic or mechanical methods, without the prior written permission of the publisher, except in the case of brief quotations embodied in critical reviews and certain other noncommercial uses permitted by copyright law.

Cover Design: Margaret Harris

DISCLAIMER

This biography of Andy Moog is based on information that is readily available to the public and on the author's observations and insights from various sources. Though every attempt has been made to guarantee that the events and details are accurate, the author's view or opinion may be reflected in some sections.

The content is neither connected to nor endorsed by Andy Moog, his family, or any related organizations; it is only provided for informational and entertainment reasons. The people, places, and dates described in the book are merely presented as examples to provide readers with a thorough grasp of Moog's life and career.

The publisher and author have tried to uphold the rights and privacy of those listed. We apologize for any mistakes or omissions. It is suggested that readers appreciate this examination of Moog's life and contributions to hockey with the knowledge that the purpose of this biography is to honour his accomplishments and tell his inspirational tale.

Images and trademarks are used without authorization. The owners of the trademarks have not approved, linked, or endorsed their use. This book contains trademarks and images used only for explanation; no attempt is made to violate the rights of the trademark owners.

TABLE OF CONTENTS

INTRODUCTION 1

Chapter 1: Early Years in Penticton 3
    Overview of Andy Moog's Childhood in Penticton, British Columbia 3
    Introduction to Hockey and Early Passion for the Sport 6
    First Experiences Playing as a Goaltender and the Influence of His Family 10
    High School Years and Development of His Goaltending Skills 15

Chapter 2: The Road to the Nhl 19
    Moog's Journey through Junior Hockey and His Performance with the Billings Bighorns 19
    The 1980 NHL Entry Draft and Being Selected by the Edmonton Oilers 22
    Transition to Professional Hockey and Initial Challenges in the NHL 25
    Making a Name for Himself as a Backup to Grant Fuhr 29

Chapter 3: The Edmonton Oilers Dynasty 33
    Role In The Oilers' Success during the 1980s 33
    Detailed Account of the Three Stanley Cup Victories (1984, 1985, 1987) 36
    Moog's Key Performances in Crucial Playoff Games 39
    Relationship and Rivalry with Grant Fuhr as a Dynamic Goaltending Duo 42

Chapter 4: A New Chapter in Boston 46
    The Trade to the Boston Bruins in 1988 and the Shift to Becoming a Starting Goaltender 46
    Immediate Impact on the Bruins' Performance and Leading them to the Stanley Cup Finals 49
    Memorable Moments and Standout Performances during His Time in Boston 53
    The Challenge of Facing His Former Team, the Oilers, in the 1990 Stanley Cup Finals 56

Chapter 5: Consistency in Dallas 60
    Moog's Move to the Dallas Stars and His Role as a Veteran Leader 60
    The Importance of His Stability and Experience in a Young, Developing Team ... 62
    Contribution to the Stars' Rise as a Competitive Force in the NHL 65
    Key Games and Moments that Solidified His Reputation in Dallas 67

Chapter 6: Closing Out With the Montreal Canadiens 71
    The Final Phase of Moog's Playing Career with the Montreal Canadiens 71

Adapting to a New Team Environment and Maintaining Performance as a Seasoned Goaltender *74*

Reflections on His Career as He Approached Retirement *77*

The Decision to Step away From Playing Professional Hockey *81*

Chapter 7: Transitioning to Coaching and Mentorship 85

Moog's Shift from Player to Goaltending Coach and Mentor *85*

His Coaching Philosophy and Approach to Developing the Next Generation of Goaltenders *88*

Roles with Various NHL Teams and Contributions to their Success *91*

Impact on Young Goalies and His Legacy as a Teacher of the Game *95*

Chapter 8: The Legacy of a Hockey Icon 99

Analysis of Andy Moog's Playing Style, Strengths, And Influence on the Goaltending Position . *99*

His Reputation as a Reliable, Calm, and Consistent Presence in the Net *102*

The Respect and Admiration He Earned From Teammates, Opponents, and Fans *105*

Awards, Honors, and Recognition throughout His Career *107*

Chapter 9: Off the Ice: The Man behind the Mask 109

Insights into Moog's Personality, Character, And Life Away From Hockey *109*

His Involvement in Charitable Activities and Community Work *111*

The Balance between Family Life and a Demanding Hockey Career *113*

Reflections from Friends, Family, And Colleagues on Moog's Impact off the Ice *115*

Chapter 10: Reflections and Enduring Influence 119

Moog's Thoughts on His Career, The Lessons Learned, and the Moments That Defined Him .. *119*

The Lasting Influence of Andy Moog on the Sport of Hockey and Future Generations of Goaltenders *122*

Reflections on How His Story Continues to Inspire Players and Fans Alike *125*

Final Thoughts on His Legacy as a Pillar of Success and Stability in the World of Hockey *128*

CONCLUSION 132

INTRODUCTION

In the annals of hockey history, few players have left as enduring a legacy as Andy Moog. As a goaltender who graced the ice for over a decade, his career is a story of excellence, dedication, and a deep love for the sport. This book delves into the life and career of a man whose name is synonymous with reliability and calm under pressure, who excelled in the crease and contributed significantly to the game off the ice.

Moog's journey in professional hockey is one of remarkable achievements, marked by numerous playoff appearances, Stanley Cup victories, and an unwavering commitment to his craft. However, this book is not just a recounting of statistics and milestones. It explores the man behind the mask, the values that guided him, and his impact on those around him. From his early days learning the game to his transition into coaching and mentorship, Moog's story is one of passion and perseverance that continues to inspire players and fans alike.

The narrative of Moog's life is intertwined with the evolution of the goaltending position itself. As the sport advanced, so did the techniques and strategies employed by those tasked with guarding the net. Moog was at the forefront of these changes, adapting his style and refining his approach to remain competitive in an ever-evolving game. His ability to anticipate plays, quick reflexes, and mental fortitude made him a formidable presence in the net, earning him the respect and admiration of teammates and opponents alike. This book provides an in-depth look at how Moog's approach to goaltending helped shape the modern game and set new standards for those who followed in his footsteps.

Yet, Moog's influence extends beyond the ice. His role as a mentor and coach has allowed him to pass on his knowledge to a new generation of goaltenders. This book explores how he has nurtured young talent, imparting lessons not only on technique but also on the game's mental aspects. His coaching philosophy, rooted in the importance of preparation, consistency, and resilience, has left an indelible mark on the players he has guided. Through his work with various NHL teams, Moog has contributed to the success of many and has ensured that his legacy will endure long after his playing days have ended.

In writing this book, the aim is to provide readers with a comprehensive understanding of Andy Moog's contributions to hockey. His story is not just about individual success but about teamwork, leadership, and the drive to be the best, not for personal glory but for the team's benefit. Moog's career is a reminder of the importance of humility and the recognition that, while individual accolades are significant, collective achievements define a true champion.

This introduction is the gateway to a deeper exploration of Andy Moog's life and career. Each chapter will take you through different phases of his journey, offering insights into his experiences, challenges, and the moments that defined him. Whether you are a long-time hockey fan, a player looking for inspiration, or someone new to the sport, this book offers something for everyone. It is a celebration of a career well played and a life well lived, a tribute to a man who gave everything he had to the game he loves.

As you turn these pages, you will learn not only about Andy Moog, the player, but also about Andy Moog, the mentor, the leader, and the person. His story is one of resilience, growth, and the pursuit of excellence, which continues to inspire both within the hockey community and beyond.

Chapter 1: Early Years in Penticton

Overview of Andy Moog's Childhood in Penticton, British Columbia

Andy Moog was born on February 18, 1960, in Penticton, British Columbia, a small town in the picturesque Okanagan Valley. Penticton, with its stunning landscapes of rolling hills, vineyards, and pristine lakes, provided a serene and supportive environment for young Andy as he grew up. The town, known for its close-knit community and love of outdoor activities, profoundly influenced Moog's early years, shaping his character and instilling in him the values of hard work, perseverance, and humility.

Moog's family played a significant role in his upbringing. His parents, deeply rooted in the community, encouraged him to explore various interests and supported his early endeavours. The Moog household was a place of warmth, where values such as respect, responsibility, and dedication were taught and lived. His father, a man of strong principles, was particularly influential, providing guidance and serving as a role model for Andy. It was from his father that Moog learned the importance of maintaining a calm demeanour, a trait that would later become one of his trademarks on the ice.

The community of Penticton was sports-oriented, with hockey holding a special place in the hearts of its residents. Like many Canadian towns, Penticton's winters were synonymous with ice hockey. Local rinks buzzed with activity, and children spent countless hours skating, playing pick-up games, and dreaming of one day making it to the NHL. Moog was no exception. He was drawn to the sport from an early age and captivated by the speed, skill, and excitement that hockey offered. His first pair of skates, a modest hand-me-down, began a lifelong passion.

Moog's introduction to organized hockey came through the Penticton Minor Hockey Association, a community-driven organization that nurtured young talent. Like many of his peers, he started playing as a forward, but it didn't take long for him to find his true calling between the pipes. The transition to goaltending happened almost serendipitously. The team's regular goalie was absent during a practice session, and young Andy volunteered to step in. Despite the awkwardness and the oversized equipment, Moog felt an instant connection to the position. The challenge of being the last line of defence, the pressure of protecting the net, and the unique skill set required to be a goaltender resonated with him.

As Moog's interest in goaltending grew, he devoted more time to mastering the craft. His parents recognized his passion and did everything they could to support it despite the financial strains of purchasing goalie equipment, which was significantly more expensive than the gear needed for other positions. The Moog family's commitment to Andy's dreams was unwavering, and they often made sacrifices to ensure he had what he needed to succeed.

A steep learning curve marked Moog's early experiences with goals. The position required quick reflexes, mental toughness, and the ability to read the game, skills Moog was determined to develop. He spent countless hours on the ice, practising his stance, improving his glove hand, and honing his ability to track the puck. His dedication did not go unnoticed. Coaches and teammates alike were impressed by his work ethic and calm, focused demeanour, even during the most intense game moments. These qualities would become hallmarks of his playing style in the future.

Off the ice, Moog was a typical small-town kid. He enjoyed the simple pleasures that life in Penticton offered, from fishing in Okanagan Lake to hiking in the surrounding hills. The outdoors played a significant role in his upbringing, providing him with a sense of peace and a connection to nature that remained with him throughout his life. His love for his hometown and its natural beauty was evident in his pride in representing Penticton wherever his hockey career took him.

Education was also a priority in the Moog household. Despite his growing commitment to hockey, Moog understood the importance of balancing academics with sports. He attended Pen High, the local high school, where he was known as a diligent student who excelled both in the classroom and on the ice. His teachers often remarked on his ability to remain composed and focused, qualities that were reflected in his academic performance. The discipline he learned through his studies complemented his training regimen, helping him to develop the mental toughness necessary to succeed as a goaltender.

As Moog progressed through youth hockey ranks, his talent became increasingly apparent. He was known for his quick reflexes, sharp instincts, and the ability to stay calm under pressure. These attributes set him apart from his peers and caught the attention of local coaches. His reputation as a promising young goaltender spread beyond Penticton, leading to opportunities to play at higher levels of competition. Despite his success, Moog remained humble, grounded by the values instilled in him by his family and the supportive community that had nurtured his development.

By the time Moog reached his mid-teens, it was clear that he had the potential to pursue a hockey career. However, the path to the NHL was fraught with challenges. The competition was fierce, and only a select few would make it to the professional level. Moog was well aware of the odds but was undeterred. He was driven by a love for the game and a desire to push himself to be the best he could be.

Moog's first major break came when he joined the Billings Bighorns of the Western Hockey League (WHL). The move marked a significant step up in competition and presented new challenges for the young goaltender. He was now playing against some of the best junior players in the country, many of whom would go on to have successful careers in the NHL. The experience was both daunting and exhilarating, as it gave Moog a taste of what it would take to succeed at the highest levels of the sport.

Despite the pressures of playing in the WHL, Moog never lost sight of where he came from. He often reflected on his childhood in Penticton and the lessons he had learned along the way. The work ethic, discipline, and resilience instilled in him during his early years continued to guide him as he navigated the ups and downs of his hockey career. Moog remained close to his family, often returning home during the off-season to reconnect with his roots and recharge before another gruelling hockey campaign started.

Moog's upbringing in Penticton also influenced his approach to the mental aspect of goaltending. He understood the importance of staying mentally sharp and focused, which is crucial for a position demanding physical and psychological resilience. The calm, measured demeanour he displayed on the ice reflected the steady, supportive environment in which he was raised. This mental toughness would prove invaluable throughout his career, allowing him to perform consistently under pressure and to rebound from setbacks with grace and determination.

As Moog's career progressed, the lessons he had learned during his childhood in Penticton remained with him. They served as a foundation upon which he built a career marked by success, stability, and a quiet confidence that earned him the respect of teammates, coaches, and fans. Moog's journey from a small-town kid with big dreams to an NHL goaltending icon is a testament.

Introduction to Hockey and Early Passion for the Sport

Andy Moog's introduction to hockey was as natural as the changing of seasons in his hometown of Penticton. From a young age, he was immersed in a culture where the sport was more than just a pastime; it was a way of life. The local rink was a central gathering place where families bonded over the excitement of games, and children, eager to emulate their heroes, laced up their skates as soon as they could walk. For Moog, hockey has become a part of his identity from his earliest moments on the ice.

The first time Moog stepped onto the ice was an experience that left an indelible mark on him. His initial attempts at skating were unsteady, marked by wobbles and falls typical for any beginner. But there was a spark, an immediate fascination with the feel of the ice beneath his blades, the crisp air, and the echoing sounds of pucks hitting sticks. These early experiences were not about skill or competition but rather a pure, unfiltered joy. The rink became a place of endless possibilities, where he could lose himself in the rhythm of skating and the exhilaration of movement.

As he spent more time on the ice, Moog's connection to hockey deepened. He was drawn to the game's speed, the strategy involved, and the camaraderie it fostered among players. Watching older boys play, he observed the intensity they competed, the skill required to manoeuvre the puck, and the importance of teamwork. These observations fueled his desire to learn and improve. He quickly progressed from merely skating to picking up a stick, eager to participate in the game, captivating his imagination.

Moog's early passion for hockey was nurtured by the environment he grew up in. Like many Canadian towns, Penticton revered its hockey players, and local games were community events that drew spectators of all ages. The town's pride in its hockey tradition was palpable, and Moog was keenly aware of the legacy he was stepping into. He attended games at the local arena, watching with wide-eyed excitement as players demonstrated the skills he hoped to possess. These experiences at the rink were formative, planting the seeds of ambition and a deep love for the game.

The backyard rink became crucial to Moog's development as a young player. During the long Canadian winters, Moog's father would flood the yard, creating a makeshift rink where Andy could practice endlessly. On this rink, Moog honed his skating, stickhandling, and shooting skills, often playing until the cold drove him indoors. These sessions were not disciplined or structured; they expressed his growing love for hockey. He spent hours imagining scenarios, pretending to be his favourite players, and scoring the game-winning goal. The backyard rink was a sanctuary where he could experiment, make mistakes, and learn at his own pace.

A deep admiration also marked Moog's early years for professional hockey players. He closely followed the careers of NHL stars, watching games on television whenever he could and studying the techniques of the goaltenders he admired. Players like Ken Dryden, whose calm, composed style in net became legendary, were among his early inspirations. Moog was particularly drawn to being a goaltender, fascinated by the position's unique challenges. The responsibility of being the last line of defence appealed to him, as did the mental toughness required to perform under pressure.

The community leagues in Penticton offered Moog his first taste of organized hockey. Playing with peers, he began understanding the importance of teamwork, strategy, and discipline. The games were competitive but also a source of immense joy. Moog loved the thrill of competition, the way the game demanded both physical and mental agility. His natural athleticism became apparent during these early games, and his quick reflexes and sharp instincts set him apart from other players his age. Coaches took notice of his potential, encouraging him to continue developing his skills.

As his passion for the sport grew, so did his commitment to improvement. Moog was not content with participating; he wanted to excel. This drive led him to seek out additional opportunities to play and practice. Whether it was during organized team practices, pick-up games with friends, or solo sessions on the backyard rink, Moog was constantly pushing himself. He understood that hockey was a game of inches, where small improvements could make a significant difference. This mindset would stay with him throughout his career, fueling his relentless pursuit of excellence.

The technical aspects of goaltending fascinated Moog. He became a student of the game, eager to learn everything he could about the position. He paid close attention to the fundamentals: positioning, angles, and the art of making saves. Beyond physical skills, Moog was also drawn to the psychological aspect of goaltending. He understood early on that a goaltender needed to be mentally resilient, stay calm in the face of intense pressure and bounce back from setbacks quickly. These were qualities he worked on from a young age, building the mental fortitude that would later become one of his greatest strengths.

Moog's early experiences in hockey were also shaped by the friendships he made on the ice. The bonds formed with teammates during these formative years were strong and enduring. They shared a common goal, a passion for the sport, and a willingness to work hard to improve. The sense of camaraderie and mutual respect that developed during these years was one of the most rewarding aspects of playing hockey for Moog. The friendships extended beyond the rink, as they spent time together off the ice, talking about hockey, practising their skills, and dreaming of future successes.

The support of Moog's family was a constant source of encouragement. His parents recognized his passion for hockey and did everything they could to support his development. Whether driving him to early morning practices, cheering him on from the stands, or investing in the necessary equipment, they were fully committed to helping him achieve his goals. Their belief in his abilities and their willingness to make sacrifices so he could pursue his dream were powerful motivators for Moog. He knew that his success on the ice was a personal achievement and a reflection of their unwavering support.

As Moog continued progressing in his hockey journey, his passion for the game deepened. He became more focused and more determined to succeed. The thrill of stopping a breakaway, the satisfaction of a well-executed save, and the rush of victory fueled his desire to keep improving. Hockey was no longer just a hobby; it had become integral to who he was. Every practice, every game, and every challenge he faced on the ice was an opportunity to grow, to push his limits, and to inch closer to his dream of playing at the highest level.

The transition from playing for fun to pursuing hockey with a serious, competitive edge was gradual for Moog. There was no single moment when he decided that hockey was his future; instead, it was a series of small steps, each building on the last that led him down that path. As he advanced through the youth hockey ranks, he began to see the possibilities ahead. His talent was undeniable, and with it came opportunities to play at higher levels of competition. The prospect of turning his passion into a career was becoming increasingly realistic.

Throughout these early years, Moog's love for hockey never waned. The sport gave him a sense of purpose, a challenge he was eager to meet head-on. His passion was evident in how he approached every aspect of the game, from his meticulous preparation to his fierce competitiveness on the ice. Hockey had captured his heart from that first moment on the ice, and it would remain a driving force in his life for years to come. As he continued to develop his skills and gain experience, it became clear that Andy Moog was destined for greatness in the sport he loved.

First Experiences Playing as a Goaltender and the Influence of His Family

Andy Moog's journey into the crease as a goaltender began somewhat serendipitously, but it quickly became evident that this was where he was meant to be. His first experiences playing as a goaltender were shaped by a combination of curiosity, determination, and a strong familial influence that supported and nurtured his budding talent.

Moog's introduction to goaltending occurred during a local pick-up game. At the time, he was still finding his place on the ice, experimenting with different positions to understand where he felt most comfortable. During one game, the team found itself without a goaltender, and Moog, eager to contribute, volunteered to stand in the net. This decision was not deliberate but rather a spur-of-the-moment choice driven by his desire to be involved in every aspect of the game. As he pulled on the pads, something clicked. The role felt natural, almost automatic, and as the game progressed, Moog found himself thriving under the pressure.

The first few shots that came his way were a mixture of excitement and nerves. Moog had always admired the goaltenders he watched, appreciating their ability to change the course of a game with a single save. As he faced the opposing players, he experienced that sensation firsthand. The satisfaction of stopping a shot was unlike anything he had felt before. The concentration required to track the puck, anticipate the shooter's next move and react in time to make the save was exhilarating. By the end of the game, Moog knew he had found his calling.

As Moog began to play more regularly as a goaltender, he quickly realized that the position was far more challenging than he had imagined. It required physical agility, sharp reflexes, mental grit, and resilience. He took to these challenges enthusiastically, viewing each game and practice as an opportunity to improve. The more he played, the more he understood the nuances of goaltending: the importance of positioning, reading the play, and maintaining focus even when the puck was at the other end of the ice. These early lessons were invaluable, laying the groundwork for the disciplined and strategic approach that defined his career.

The role of his family during this formative period was crucial. Moog's parents, who had always supported his hockey ambitions, quickly recognised his affinity for goaltending. They saw the spark in his eyes when he talked about the position, the way he eagerly looked forward to every opportunity to play in the net. Understanding the significance of nurturing their son's passion, they did everything they could to support him. This support ranged from practical matters, such as purchasing the necessary equipment, to more emotional and psychological encouragement, offering words of motivation after both victories and defeats.

Moog's father, in particular, played a significant role in his early development as a goaltender. A sports enthusiast himself, he understood the mental demands of the position. He spent countless hours with Andy, discussing the game, offering advice, and helping him develop the mindset needed to succeed in such a high-pressure role. Whether breaking down plays, discussing strategies, or simply providing a listening ear after a tough game, his father was a constant source of guidance and wisdom. This father-son bond became a cornerstone of Moog's early career, instilling in him the values of perseverance, hard work, and a positive attitude.

The backyard rink, which had already been a place of joy for young Andy, now took on an even greater significance. It became his training ground, where he could refine his goaltending skills away from the pressures of organized games. His father often joined him on the ice, shooting pucks and helping him practice different scenarios. These sessions were challenging and fun, fostering a deep connection between them while allowing Andy to improve his game in a supportive environment. The rink was a place of learning, where mistakes were simply part of the process, and every save was a step closer to mastering the craft.

Moog's siblings also played a role in his development, often joining him for impromptu games on the backyard rink. These games were more than just practice; they were a source of camaraderie and friendly competition that pushed Andy to improve. His siblings played as shooters, testing his reflexes with every shot. These sessions were informal yet intense, filled with laughter and the occasional argument typical of sibling rivalry. Through these interactions, Andy developed his technical skills and the mental toughness required to handle the pressures of being a goaltender. His siblings, in their own way, became his first real competitors, challenging him to improve with each shot.

As Moog continued to play in more formal settings, his natural talent as a goaltender became increasingly apparent. Coaches began to take notice of the young player, who seemed to have an innate ability to read the game and make crucial saves under pressure. His quick reflexes and his growing understanding of the position made him stand out among his peers. It wasn't long before Moog was encouraged to focus exclusively on goaltending, a suggestion he enthusiastically welcomed. The position had captured his heart, and he was eager to dedicate himself fully to mastering it.

One of the most significant aspects of Moog's early experiences as a goaltender was the support network that surrounded him. His family's unwavering belief in his abilities gave him the confidence to pursue his dreams without hesitation. Their encouragement helped him navigate the inevitable challenges of such a demanding position. Whether it was a tough loss or a period of self-doubt, Moog knew he could rely on his family for support and guidance. This support extended beyond just the immediate family, with extended relatives and friends also playing a part in cheering him on, attending games, and celebrating his achievements.

The influence of his family went beyond just moral support. They helped him develop a balanced perspective on both hockey and life. His parents emphasized the importance of education, ensuring that Andy understood the value of academics even as he pursued his hockey dreams. This balance between sports and education was crucial in shaping Moog into a well-rounded individual who could handle the pressures of the game while maintaining a grounded outlook on life. The lessons he learned during this period would serve him well throughout his career, helping him navigate the ups and downs of professional sports with grace and resilience.

As Moog's commitment to goaltending deepened, his family made sacrifices to ensure he had the best opportunities to develop his skills. They invested in quality equipment, understanding that having the right gear was essential for performance and safety. They also rearranged their schedules to accommodate his practices, games, and travel for tournaments. These sacrifices were made without hesitation, driven by their belief in Andy's potential and their desire to see him succeed. This unwavering support was humbling and motivating for Moog, pushing him to work even harder to achieve his goals.

Through these early experiences, Moog began understanding the responsibilities of being a goaltender. He was no longer just another player on the ice; he was the last line of defence his team relied on to make the big saves. This realization brought with it a sense of pride, purpose, and determination to be the best he could be. Moog embraced the challenge, eager to prove himself and earn the trust of his teammates and coaches. Every game was an opportunity to learn, grow, and solidify his place between the pipes.

As the years passed, Moog's experiences as a young goaltender laid the foundation for a storied career. The lessons learned during those early days about perseverance, resilience, and the importance of support stayed with him throughout his journey. His family's influence was a constant source of strength, helping him navigate the challenges of professional hockey with the same determination and passion that had driven him from the start. The journey from those tentative steps in the net to becoming a pillar of stability and success was marked by hard work, dedication, and an unwavering belief in the power of a supportive family.

High School Years and Development of His Goaltending Skills

Andy Moog's high school years marked a critical period in his development as a goaltender. As he entered adolescence, the stakes grew higher, and the demands of balancing academics, social life, and his commitment to hockey became increasingly challenging. Yet, during this time, Moog's skills between the pipes began to mature, setting the stage for his future success in the sport.

Moog attended Pen-Hi, short for Penticton Secondary School, where sports were a significant part of the culture. The school had a strong athletic program, and hockey was among the most revered sports. For Moog, the opportunity to represent his school on the ice was both an honour and a responsibility. The competition was fierce, with many talented players vying for positions on the team. As he transitioned into high school, he was determined to secure his spot as the starting goaltender, knowing this was the next crucial step in his hockey journey.

The rigours of high school life did little to diminish Moog's dedication to hockey. Despite the demands of his academic schedule, he made time for early-morning practices and late-night games. His days were often long, filled with classes, homework, and hours spent on the ice or in the gym. This commitment required physical endurance and a high level of discipline. Moog learned to manage his time effectively, prioritizing his responsibilities and making sacrifices when necessary. His focus was unwavering; he knew every practice, every drill, and every game was an opportunity to refine his craft.

During this period, Moog's goaltending skills underwent significant refinement. High school hockey presented new challenges, with faster-paced games and more skilled opponents than he had previously faced. Moog quickly realized that his reflexes and positioning alone would not be enough; he needed to develop a deeper understanding of the game, anticipate plays before they happened, and maintain a strong mental game throughout each match. These were lessons learned through experience, as Moog faced various offensive threats that tested his abilities and pushed him to improve.

A key aspect of Moog's development was his growing understanding of the technical side of goaltending. He became increasingly aware of the importance of positioning, learning to cut down angles and control rebounds. This period of growth involved countless hours spent studying the game, both on the ice and off. Moog watched other goaltenders closely, analyzing their techniques and adapting what he learned to his style of play. He focused on refining his butterfly-style lateral movement and improving his glove hand. These skills became the foundation of his goaltending, allowing him to remain calm and composed under pressure.

The mental aspect of goaltending also took on greater significance during Moog's high school years. He began to understand that a goaltender's success was as much about mental toughness as physical skill. Games often hinged on a single save or a momentary lapse in concentration. Moog learned to maintain his focus throughout the game, even when the action was at the other end of the ice. He developed routines and mental exercises to help him stay sharp, such as visualization techniques and controlled breathing. These practices helped him remain calm in high-pressure situations, a trait that would become one of his trademarks.

Moog's high school coach played a pivotal role in his development. Recognizing Moog's potential, the coach worked closely with him, offering guidance and feedback that helped him elevate his game. Under his coach's tutelage, Moog learned to analyze his performance critically, identifying areas where he could improve and setting goals. This self-awareness became a driving force behind his growth as a goaltender. The coach also emphasized the importance of teamwork, teaching Moog how to communicate effectively with his defensemen and work as a cohesive unit. This understanding of the team dynamic was essential, as it allowed Moog to build trust with his teammates and establish himself as a reliable last line of defence.

Off the ice, Moog's commitment to hockey influenced his social life as well. While many of his peers spent their free time hanging out or attending social events, Moog often found himself at the rink, either practising or preparing for upcoming games. This dedication sometimes meant missing out on typical high school experiences, but Moog had no regrets. His passion for hockey was all-consuming, and he was willing to sacrifice to pursue his dream. His friends and classmates respected his commitment, and many admired his work ethic and determination.

Despite the challenges, Moog's high school years were filled with memorable moments. He experienced the highs and lows that come with competitive sports: thrilling victories, tough losses, and the satisfaction of seeing his hard work pay off. These experiences helped him build resilience, teaching him to bounce back from setbacks and strive for improvement. Moog also cherished the camaraderie he shared with his teammates. The bonds formed in the locker room and on the ice were strong, forged through shared experiences and a mutual love for the game.

As Moog continued to hone his skills, his reputation as a top goaltender grew. He began to attract attention from scouts and coaches at higher levels of competition. This recognition was a testament to his progress during high school, a period of intense growth and development. The prospect of playing hockey at an even higher level was exciting but also brought new challenges. Moog understood that the competition would only get tougher, and he was determined to rise to the occasion.

Balancing academics with his hockey aspirations was difficult, but Moog excelled. His parents strongly emphasised education, and Moog was mindful of the importance of his studies. He approached his schoolwork with the same discipline and focus he applied to hockey, ensuring his grades remained strong. This balance between academics and athletics was crucial, as it kept Moog grounded and provided him with a well-rounded perspective. His success in school also opened doors for him, giving him the option to pursue higher education alongside his hockey career.

As Moog neared the end of his high school career, he began to consider his options for the future. He had always dreamed of playing professional hockey but also recognized the value of a solid education. The decision-making process was not easy, as he weighed the risks and rewards of each path. His family was instrumental in helping him navigate this period, offering advice and support as he considered his options. Moog's parents encouraged him to keep all doors open, reminding him that education and hockey could go hand in hand.

By the time Moog graduated from high school, he was a well-rounded and highly skilled goaltender. His experiences over the previous years had shaped him into a player with both the technical ability and the mental strength needed to succeed at higher levels of competition. He had grown as a hockey player and as a person, developing qualities such as leadership, resilience, and a strong work ethic. These traits would serve him well as he embarked on the next chapter of his hockey career, taking with him the lessons learned during those formative high school years.

Andy Moog's development of goaltending skills during his high school years was a journey marked by hard work, dedication, and a relentless pursuit of excellence. The challenges he faced, both on and off the ice, helped to mould him into the goaltender and the person he would become. As he looked ahead, Moog was ready to take on whatever came next, armed with the skills and experiences that had defined his high school years.

Chapter 2: The Road to the Nhl

Moog's Journey through Junior Hockey and His Performance with the Billings Bighorns

Andy Moog's progression into junior hockey was pivotal in his development as a goaltender. Transitioning from high school hockey, Moog took his talents to the next level, where the competition was more intense and the stakes much higher. This phase of his career was defined by his time with the Billings Bighorns of the Western Canada Hockey League (WCHL), a team that provided him with the platform to showcase his abilities and hone his craft in a highly competitive environment.

The move to junior hockey represented a significant step up for Moog. Junior leagues in Canada were known for their rigorous schedules and the high calibre of players they attracted. For many young athletes, these leagues were the final proving grounds before advancing to the professional ranks. Moog understood that this was where he needed to make his mark. The transition was not challenging, as the game's speed increased and the physical demands became more pronounced. Despite these challenges, Moog approached this opportunity with the same determination and work ethic that had characterized his previous years.

Joining the Billings Bighorns, Moog quickly realized that he was now part of a league where every player was fighting to be noticed by scouts and professional teams. The pressure was immense, but Moog thrived under it. The Bighorns were a strong team with a reputation for developing talented players, and Moog was eager to contribute to their success. When he stepped onto the ice with his new team, he was determined to prove himself as a reliable and skilled goaltender.

Moog's time with the Bighorns was marked by impressive performances that highlighted his growth as a goaltender. The WCHL was a fast-paced league, and Moog quickly adapted to the players' increased speed and skill level. He refined his positioning, learning to anticipate plays more accurately and improving his ability to read the game. This period was crucial for Moog, as he developed quick reflexes and sharp mental focus, which became his trademarks.

One of the key aspects of Moog's success with the Bighorns was his ability to remain calm under pressure. Junior hockey was a tough, physical environment, and goaltenders were often the target of aggressive plays. Moog faced this challenge head-on, maintaining his composure even in the most intense situations. His poise in the crease earned him the respect of his teammates and coaches, who recognized that they could rely on him in critical moments. This mental toughness was a significant factor in Moog's ability to deliver consistent performances throughout his time with the team.

As Moog continued to develop his skills, he also gained valuable experience in dealing with the demands of a long and gruelling season. The WCHL schedule was rigorous, with numerous games played over a relatively short period. This schedule's physical and mental strain was considerable, but Moog was up to the task. He maintained a rigorous training regimen, focusing on his physical fitness to ensure he could withstand the rigours of the season. His commitment to staying in peak condition was evident in his performances, as he remained sharp and effective throughout the year.

During his time with the Bighorns, Moog was also exposed to a higher level of coaching and mentorship. The coaching staff recognized his potential and worked closely with him to refine his game. They provided him with the technical guidance he needed to improve his mechanics and the strategic insights that helped him better understand the nuances of goaltending at a higher level. This coaching was instrumental in Moog's development, allowing him to take his game to new heights and prepare for the challenges ahead.

Moog's performance with the Bighorns did not go unnoticed. His consistent play and ability to deliver under pressure caught the attention of scouts from professional teams, who began to take a serious interest in the young goaltender. This recognition was a testament to Moog's progress during his time in junior hockey. He had proven himself as a goaltender capable of competing at a high level, and his prospects for a professional career were looking increasingly promising.

The experience Moog gained with the Bighorns was invaluable. The WCHL allowed him to compete against some of the best young players in the country, pushing him to elevate his game and refine his skills. The league's fast pace and physical nature helped Moog develop the toughness and resilience that would be essential in his professional career. His time with the Bighorns also taught him the importance of consistency, as he learned to deliver high-level performances night after night, regardless of the circumstances.

Off the ice, Moog's experience with the Bighorns helped him mature as a person. Living away from home for the first time, he had to adapt to the challenges of managing his schedule and taking responsibility for his daily routine. This independence was critical to his growth, as it taught him the discipline and self-reliance necessary in the professional ranks. Moog embraced this new chapter in his life, understanding that these experiences prepared him for the future.

Moog's time with the Billings Bighorns was not just about personal development but also about contributing to his team's success. The Bighorns were a competitive team in the WCHL, and Moog played a key role in their performance during his tenure. His steady presence in the net gave his teammates confidence, knowing they had a reliable goaltender backing them up. Moog's ability to make crucial saves in tight games was a significant factor in the Bighorns' success during the season.

The camaraderie and bonds formed during his time with the Bighorns were also an important part of Moog's junior hockey experience. The close-knit nature of the team provided a support system that helped him navigate the challenges of junior hockey. The friendships he made and the experiences he shared with his teammates were memories he would carry throughout his career. This sense of belonging and the shared goal of achieving success as a team were the driving forces behind Moog's dedication to his craft. As Moog's time with the Bighorns ended, he had established himself as one of the top goaltenders in the WCHL. His performance in junior hockey had set the stage for the next phase of his career, where he would take on even greater challenges in pursuing his dream of playing professional hockey. The skills, experience, and mental toughness he developed during his time with the Bighorns would serve him well as he continued his journey toward the NHL. Moog had laid a solid foundation and was ready to take the next step in his hockey career.

The 1980 NHL Entry Draft and Being Selected by the Edmonton Oilers

The 1980 NHL Entry Draft was a significant moment in Andy Moog's career, marking the transition from his junior hockey years to the professional stage. Moog had spent years honing his skills and demonstrating his potential, and the draft represented the culmination of his hard work and determination. The process of being selected by a National Hockey League team was both a dream come true and a moment of intense pressure for any young player, as it set the course for their future in the sport.

For Moog, the journey to the draft was characterized by years of dedication to his craft. His time with the Billings Bighorns in the

Western Canada Hockey League had put him on the scouts' radar, and his consistent performance in the crease had made him a player to watch. The draft itself, however, was a different kind of challenge. It was a highly anticipated event, with scouts, coaches, and general managers evaluating hundreds of young players, each hoping to secure a spot in the NHL. The stakes were incredibly high, and the competition was fierce.

As the draft approached, Moog knew that his chances of being selected were good, but there were no guarantees. The NHL was filled with talented goaltenders, and teams were looking for players who could not only perform at a high level but also had the potential to develop into long-term assets for their organizations. Moog's strengths as a goaltender, including his quick reflexes, sharp mental focus, and ability to remain calm under pressure, made him an attractive prospect. Yet, he knew many factors could influence where or if he would be drafted.

The day of the 1980 NHL Entry Draft arrived, and it was a nerve-wracking experience for Moog and his family. The draft occurred at the Montreal Forum, one of the most iconic arenas in hockey history. The atmosphere was charged with anticipation as young players and their families waited anxiously to hear their names called. For Moog, it was the culmination of years of hard work and dedication, and the uncertainty of the draft only heightened the emotional intensity of the moment.

As the draft progressed, the Edmonton Oilers, a relatively new franchise in the NHL, were making their selections. The Oilers were building a team that would become one of the most dominant in NHL history, but at the time, they were still assembling the pieces that would make up their championship core. The team's management, led by General Manager Glen Sather, was keen on finding young talent to contribute to their long-term success. The Oilers were particularly interested in building a strong, reliable goaltending corps to support their high-powered offence.

When the Oilers' selection in the seventh round came up, they called out the name "Andy Moog." For Moog, hearing his name was an extraordinary moment he had dreamed of for years. Being drafted into the NHL was a recognition of his skills and potential and the opportunity he had been working towards throughout his junior career. The fact that the Oilers, a team with such promise and ambition, had chosen him made the moment even more special. It was the beginning of a new chapter in his life that would bring both challenges and triumphs.

The Oilers' decision to draft Moog was based on their assessment of his abilities and potential. They saw in him a goaltender who could develop into a key player for their team. Moog's style of play, characterized by his agility, quick reactions, and strong mental game, aligned well with the Oilers' fast-paced, aggressive approach to hockey. The team was confident Moog could provide stability in the net, a crucial factor as they sought to establish themselves as contenders in the NHL.

After being drafted, Moog's journey was far from over. Being selected in the draft was just the beginning; he had to prove himself in training camp and earn a spot on the Oilers' roster. The NHL was a significant step up from junior hockey, and Moog knew that the transition would require him to adapt quickly to the higher level of play. He knew that his performance in the months following the draft would be critical in determining his future with the team.

Moog's selection by the Oilers also placed him in the company of some of the most talented players of his generation. The team was already home to a young Wayne Gretzky, who would become one of the greatest players in NHL history, along with other rising stars like Mark Messier and Jari Kurri. The Oilers were on the cusp of greatness, and being part of this group was an exciting and daunting prospect for Moog. He was joining a team with high expectations and a clear vision for success, and he was eager to contribute to their efforts.

The Oilers' management had high hopes for Moog, and their belief in his potential gave him the confidence to push himself even harder. He was determined to make the most of this opportunity, knowing that he was now part of a team with the potential to achieve great things. The draft had opened the door to the NHL, but it was Moog's responsibility to walk through it and prove that he belonged at the sport's highest level.

After the draft, Moog immediately began preparing for the challenges ahead. Transitioning to professional hockey required intense physical and mental preparation, and Moog was committed to making the necessary adjustments. He focused on improving his conditioning, refining his technical skills, and studying the game at a deeper level. Moog understood that the NHL was a league where even the smallest details could make a significant difference, and he was determined to leave no stone unturned in his quest to succeed.

Moog's selection by the Oilers in the 1980 NHL Entry Draft was pivotal in his career. It marked the beginning of his professional journey and set the stage for a remarkable tenure with one of the greatest teams in NHL history. The draft was a testament to Moog's hard work, dedication, and talent, and it allowed him to achieve his dreams of playing in the NHL. For Moog, being drafted by the Edmonton Oilers was not just an achievement; it was the start of an adventure that would make him a key figure in the team's rise to glory.

Transition to Professional Hockey and Initial Challenges in the NHL

Transitioning from junior hockey to the NHL is a daunting leap for any player, and it was no different for Andy Moog. After being drafted by the Edmonton Oilers in 1980, Moog found himself on the cusp of a professional career. The NHL was a league filled with seasoned veterans, each faster, stronger, and more skilled than the opponents he had faced in junior hockey. The challenge ahead was immense, but it was one that Moog approached with determination and an unwavering focus on his goal of establishing himself as a reliable goaltender in the league.

The first significant adjustment Moog had to make was adapting to the pace of the NHL. The speed of the game was unlike anything he had experienced before. Pucks moved quicker, players reacted faster, and decisions had to be made instantly. This required a heightened level of mental acuity and physical readiness. Moog spent countless hours on the ice during training camp, improving his reflexes and sharpening his situational awareness. Every practice was an opportunity to acclimate to the faster tempo, and Moog was keenly aware that his ability to keep up would determine his place on the team.

Another challenge Moog faced was the physicality of the NHL. The league was known for its rough and aggressive style of play, and as a goaltender, Moog was often the target of opposing players crashing the net in an attempt to score. This starkly contrasted with the less physical nature of junior hockey, requiring Moog to develop a new level of toughness. He needed to learn how to hold his ground, protect his crease, and not be intimidated by the size and strength of the players coming at him. The transition was not just about being a good goaltender but also about proving that he could withstand the physical rigours of the professional game.

Moog's early days with the Oilers were also marked by the pressure of proving himself to the coaching staff and his teammates. The NHL is a results-driven league, and Moog understood that his performance in practices and games would be closely scrutinized. There was no room for error, and any mistake could cost him his position on the team. This pressure was compounded by the fact that the Oilers were an up-and-coming team with high expectations. Moog was joining a roster that included some of the most talented young players in the league, and he knew that he had to earn their trust and respect. The mental challenge of maintaining confidence while facing such scrutiny was significant, and Moog had to find a way to stay focused and positive even when things didn't go perfectly.

Another challenge Moog encountered was balancing the mental and physical demands of the NHL. The rigours of the NHL schedule were gruelling, with frequent travel, back-to-back games, and the constant pressure to perform at a high level. For a young player like Moog, this was a significant adjustment. He had to quickly learn how to manage his energy levels, maintain his conditioning, and stay mentally sharp throughout the season. The travel alone was an eye-opener; the long flights and hotel stays added a layer of fatigue that Moog had not experienced in junior hockey. Learning how to deal with these challenges was essential to his success, and it required a level of discipline and self-care that was new to him.

Despite the challenges, Moog's first NHL experiences were filled with moments of excitement and learning. Being part of the Oilers organization during this time was exhilarating, as the team was on the brink of becoming a dynasty. The presence of players like Wayne Gretzky, Mark Messier, and Paul Coffey created an environment of excellence, and Moog was inspired by their work ethic and dedication to the game. He saw firsthand what it took to be successful at the highest level, and this exposure was invaluable to his development as a professional. Moog absorbed everything he could from his teammates and coaches, always striving to improve and contribute to the team's success.

The competition for the goaltending position was another hurdle Moog had to overcome. The Oilers already had established goaltenders, and Moog knew that earning ice time would not be easy. He was determined to make the most of every opportunity, whether in practice or a game. The battle for playing time was intense, and Moog had to constantly prove that he deserved to be in the lineup. This required strong performances and the ability to handle the pressure and expectations that came with being an NHL goaltender. Moog's approach was to focus on controlling his preparation, mindset, and effort rather than being distracted by external factors.

One of the most significant challenges Moog faced during his transition was managing the ups and downs of his performance. The NHL is a league where even the best goaltenders have off nights, and for a young player like Moog, learning how to bounce back from a tough game was crucial. There were times when things didn't go as planned, and Moog had to deal with the frustration and disappointment that came with it. He quickly realized that resilience was key to success in the NHL. He needed to have a short memory, learn from his mistakes, and confidently move forward. This mental toughness was something that Moog worked on continuously, knowing that his ability to stay positive and focused would be critical to his long-term success.

As Moog navigated the early challenges of his NHL career, he also began to appreciate the importance of experience. The veterans on the Oilers' roster played a crucial role in his development, offering guidance and support as he adjusted to life in the NHL. These players had been through the same process, and their advice helped Moog to better understand what was required to succeed at this level. The mentorship he received was invaluable, and Moog was grateful for the opportunity to learn from those who had already established themselves in the league. This support network was a key factor in helping him overcome his challenges during his transition.

Moog's early years in the NHL were a period of significant growth and learning. The challenges he encountered, from adapting to the speed and physicality of the game to managing the mental demands of being a professional athlete, helped to shape him into the goaltender he would become. Each obstacle he faced was an opportunity to improve, and Moog's determination to succeed drove him to push through the difficulties. The transition to professional hockey was not easy, but it was a crucial step in Moog's journey to becoming one of the most respected goaltenders in the NHL. Through hard work, resilience, and a relentless pursuit of excellence, Moog laid the foundation for a successful career that would see him achieve great things in the years to come.

Making a Name for Himself as a Backup to Grant Fuhr

Stepping into the role of backup goaltender for the Edmonton Oilers, Andy Moog faced a unique set of challenges and opportunities that would shape his career trajectory. The 1980s Oilers were a powerhouse team, stacked with talent and on the brink of establishing one of the greatest dynasties in hockey history. For a young goaltender like Moog, being part of such an illustrious team was a privilege and a test of his abilities. His role as the backup to the phenomenal Grant Fuhr required him to demonstrate his skills, mental fortitude, and readiness to perform under pressure.

Grant Fuhr was the Oilers' starting goaltender and was widely regarded as one of the best in the game. His athleticism, quick reflexes, and ability to perform in clutch situations made him a formidable presence in the net. Moog understood from the outset that competing for ice time with Fuhr would be no easy task. Yet, rather than seeing himself as merely a secondary option, Moog viewed his position as a critical part of the team's overall success. He knew that his role required him to be always prepared, ready to step in and deliver when called upon, no matter how infrequent those opportunities might be.

The dynamic between Moog and Fuhr was one of mutual respect and professional rivalry. While Fuhr was the clear starter, Moog's presence provided the Oilers with a reliable option, ensuring that the team always had a capable goaltender, regardless of who was in the net. Moog's approach to being a backup was rooted in his understanding of the team's needs. He focused on his preparation, knowing that even as a backup, he had to be at the top of his game. His time in practice was spent honing his skills, studying opposing players' tendencies and staying mentally and physically sharp. He recognized that his opportunities to play might be sporadic, but he needed to make the most of them when they came.

One of the key aspects of Moog's time as a backup was his ability to stay mentally engaged despite not being the starter. It's easy for a backup goaltender to feel disconnected from the action, especially when watching from the bench during critical game moments. However, Moog made it a point to remain focused, treating each game as if he were the starter. He studied Fuhr's movements, how he positioned himself, and how he reacted to different situations. This helped Moog learn and improve his game and kept him mentally prepared for the moments when he would be called into action.

When Moog got the nod to start, he approached each game with purpose and determination. He understood that these opportunities were his chance to prove himself to the coaching staff, his teammates, and the fans. Despite the limited starts, Moog's performances were often stellar, showcasing his ability to step up in high-pressure situations. His calm demeanour and consistency in net earned him the respect of those around him, and he quickly became known as a reliable presence for the Oilers.

One of the most significant moments during Moog's time as a backup came during the 1983 playoffs. The Oilers were on a mission to capture their first Stanley Cup, and the pressure was immense. With Fuhr dealing with injuries, Moog was thrust into the spotlight. He responded with remarkable performances, helping the Oilers advance through the playoffs. Moog's ability to rise to the occasion under such intense circumstances cemented his reputation as a clutch performer. His poise and resilience during this period were indicative of the depth of talent that the Oilers had in net, and it underscored the importance of having a backup goaltender who could step in and perform at a high level when needed.

Moog's time as a backup was also marked by his contributions to the team's success beyond just stopping pucks. He was a supportive teammate, always ready to provide encouragement and insight to those around him. The camaraderie within the Oilers' locker room was a crucial factor in their success, and Moog played a significant role in maintaining that positive atmosphere. He understood that being a backup didn't mean he was any less important to the team's overall chemistry. His ability to stay positive, even when he wasn't playing, helped to foster a sense of unity among the players, and it was this collective spirit that propelled the Oilers to their many triumphs.

The relationship between Moog and Fuhr also played a crucial role in shaping Moog's development as a goaltender. Watching and competing with one of the best in the game pushed Moog to continually improve. The friendly competition between the two drove both goaltenders to be better, as they each knew they had to bring their best to the rink every day. Fuhr's success and work ethic served as a benchmark for Moog, and rather than being discouraged by the challenge of competing with him, Moog embraced it. He saw it as an opportunity to elevate his own game, and this mindset was instrumental in his growth during his years as a backup.

Moog's ability to stay ready and perform when called upon didn't go unnoticed by the coaching staff. The Oilers' coaching team valued Moog's reliability, knowing they had a dependable goaltender to step in and keep the team competitive. This trust was evident in the critical situations where Moog was asked to play, often in high-stakes games where the margin for error was slim. Moog thrived in these moments, and his performances often exceeded expectations, leading to some of the most memorable games of his career.

Through his time as a backup, Moog developed a reputation for being one of the best second-string goaltenders in the league. His ability to perform at a high level despite not being the regular starter was a testament to his professionalism and dedication to his craft. He set an example of what it meant to be a true team player, always ready to step in and contribute whenever his number was called. This period of his career was crucial in establishing the foundation for the success he would achieve in the years to come.

Moog's experience as a backup to Grant Fuhr was more than just a stepping stone; it was a defining period that shaped his career and prepared him for the challenges ahead. The lessons he learned, the skills he developed, and the resilience he built during this time were instrumental in his evolution as a goaltender. It was a period marked by growth, perseverance, and a deep understanding of what it takes to succeed at the sport's highest level. As a backup, Moog laid the groundwork for a career that would see him become one of the most respected goaltenders in the history of the NHL.

Chapter 3: The Edmonton Oilers Dynasty

Role In The Oilers' Success during the 1980s

During the 1980s, Andy Moog played an integral role in the Edmonton Oilers' ascent to greatness, contributing significantly to their success as one of the most dominant teams in NHL history. The Oilers, led by iconic players like Wayne Gretzky, Mark Messier, and Paul Coffey, were an offensive powerhouse. However, their achievements were also deeply rooted in the strength and stability provided by their goaltending, a department in which Moog was a crucial figure.

Moog joined the Oilers when they were on the cusp of something special. The team had abundant offensive talent, but their depth, including their goaltending tandem, set them apart. Moog's ability to share the net with Grant Fuhr, one of the premier goaltenders of the era, gave the Oilers a significant advantage. This dynamic duo allowed the Oilers to maintain a high level of performance, game in and game out, regardless of who was starting in the net. Moog's presence meant that the Oilers never had to worry about a drop in goaltending quality, even when Fuhr needed rest or was sidelined.

Moog's contribution to the Oilers' success was often showcased during the regular season, where his consistent play helped the team secure high rankings and favourable playoff positions. His ability to step into the lineup and deliver solid performances allowed the Oilers to rotate their goaltenders effectively, keeping him and Fuhr fresh for the crucial games ahead. Moog's strong work ethic and his competitive nature ensured that he was always prepared to perform at a high level, whether during a stretch of consecutive starts or filling in sporadically throughout the season.

One of the defining aspects of Moog's role was his adaptability. The Oilers were known for their high-octane offence, which often meant that their goaltenders had to be prepared for extended periods without much action, only to face sudden, high-pressure situations when the opposing team launched a counterattack. Moog excelled in this environment, showing an ability to stay mentally sharp and make key saves at critical moments. His focus and composure under pressure were vital to the Oilers' ability to play their aggressive style without sacrificing defensive stability.

Moog's performances in the playoffs were especially significant to the Oilers' success. The Stanley Cup playoffs are a gruelling test of endurance and skill, and the ability to rely on more than one goaltender can be the difference between winning and losing. Moog often found himself stepping into the spotlight during these intense postseason battles, and his play was nothing short of exceptional. Whether it was in relief of Fuhr or starting in pivotal games, Moog delivered when it mattered most, helping the Oilers secure victories in critical situations.

One of the most memorable examples of Moog's impact came during the Oilers' first Stanley Cup run in 1984. Moog provided stability in the net throughout the playoffs, delivering key performances that helped the Oilers advance through the rounds. His contribution was instrumental in securing the team's first Stanley Cup, a milestone that marked the beginning of a dynasty. Moog's ability to perform at such a high level during the most pressure-filled moments of the season underscored his value to the team.

Moog's role extended beyond his on-ice performances. He was a team player in every sense, contributing to the Oilers' locker room dynamic with his positive attitude and professionalism. The camaraderie within the Oilers' roster was key to their success. Moog's ability to support his teammates, whether in the net or not, was crucial to maintaining morale and focus. His willingness to share the load with Fuhr without letting ego or competition affect their relationship was a testament to his character and commitment to the team's success.

The Oilers' coaching staff recognized Moog's importance to the team, often turning to him during challenging periods of the season or in crucial playoff series. His reliability meant that the Oilers could trust him to deliver in any situation, and this trust was repaid time and again with outstanding performances. Moog's ability to stay prepared, even when his playing time was uncertain, demonstrated his professionalism and understanding of what it took to win at the highest level.

Moog's influence on the Oilers' success during the 1980s cannot be overstated. He was a key figure in one of the greatest teams ever assembled, providing the stability and consistency in the net that allowed the Oilers to play their aggressive style of hockey. His contributions were often underappreciated compared to the offensive superstars he played with. However, those within the organization and those who closely followed the team knew just how vital Moog was to their achievements.

As the Oilers continued to rack up championships, Moog's legacy grew. He was part of three Stanley Cup-winning teams with Edmonton, each playing a crucial role in the team's success. His ability to perform under pressure, consistency, and team-first mentality were all hallmarks of his time with the Oilers. Even after he left the team, Moog's influence remained, as he had set a standard for being a reliable and unselfish goaltender on a championship team.

Moog's role in the Oilers' success during the 1980s was defined by his net excellence and ability to thrive in a high-pressure environment. He was more than just a backup; he was a cornerstone of the team's defensive strategy and a key contributor to their championship pedigree. His legacy as a member of the Oilers' dynasty is cemented by the rings he won and by the vital role he played in one of the most dominant teams the NHL has ever seen.

Detailed Account of the Three Stanley Cup Victories (1984, 1985, 1987)

Andy Moog's journey through the Edmonton Oilers' three Stanley Cup victories in 1984, 1985, and 1987 is a testament to his resilience, skill, and vital role within a team stacked with some of the greatest players in hockey history. These championships were marked by intense competition, gruelling series, and moments where Moog's contributions were indispensable to the Oilers' success.

The 1984 Stanley Cup marked the first championship in Edmonton Oilers' history, a victory that solidified the team's status as a powerhouse in the NHL. The Oilers entered the playoffs that year with high expectations, having finished the regular season as the top team in the Campbell Conference. Their journey to the Cup was challenging, as they faced formidable opponents in every round. Moog played a crucial role during the regular season, providing solid goaltending and giving Grant Fuhr the rest needed to stay fresh for the playoffs.

As the Oilers advanced through the postseason, Moog's reliability became increasingly important. The team faced the Calgary Flames in the Smythe Division Finals, a series that tested their mettle. Calgary's aggressive play and physicality required the Oilers to be sharp defensively, and Moog was called upon to step in when needed. His performance in relief of Fuhr during critical moments provided the stability the team needed to overcome their provincial rivals. The Oilers eventually won the series, setting the stage for their first appearance in the Stanley Cup Final.

The Oilers faced the New York Islanders, who had won the previous four Stanley Cups. The Islanders were a dynasty in their own right, and their experience in the playoffs made them a formidable opponent. However, the Oilers, driven by their youth, speed, and offensive firepower, were up to the challenge. The series was hard-fought, with Moog playing a key role in supporting the team's defensive efforts. The Oilers defeated the Islanders in five games, capturing their first Stanley Cup. Moog's contribution to the victory, though often overshadowed by the team's offensive stars, was critical in ensuring the Oilers' defensive resilience throughout the playoffs.

The 1985 Stanley Cup run saw the Oilers again at the NHL's pinnacle. The team had gained invaluable experience from their previous championship, and they entered the playoffs with confidence. Moog, who had continued to share goaltending duties with Fuhr during the regular season, remained an essential part of the team's success. His ability to step in and perform at a high level whenever called upon was crucial as the Oilers navigated through another tough postseason.

One of the standout moments of the 1985 playoffs was the Oilers' series against the Chicago Blackhawks in the Campbell Conference Final. Chicago was a physical team with a strong forecheck, putting constant pressure on the Oilers' defence. Moog's presence in the net was invaluable as he made several key saves during the series, helping to prevent Chicago from gaining momentum. His calm demeanour and quick reflexes were on full display, earning him praise from teammates and coaches.

The Oilers advanced to the Stanley Cup Final, facing the Philadelphia Flyers. The Flyers, known for their physical style of play, presented a challenge different from the Islanders the previous year. The series was intense, with both teams battling hard for every inch of the ice. Moog's ability to handle the pressure was evident as he provided crucial support in the net, allowing the Oilers to play their fast-paced, offensive game without fear of defensive breakdowns. The Oilers won the series in five games, securing their second consecutive Stanley Cup. As in the previous year, Moog's role in this victory was significant, as his steady goaltending helped the team maintain their dominance.

The 1987 Stanley Cup run was perhaps the most challenging of the three championships. The Oilers had established themselves as the team to beat, and every opponent they faced was eager to dethrone them. Now a seasoned veteran, Moog was instrumental throughout the regular season, once again sharing goaltending duties with Fuhr. His ability to provide reliable goaltending allowed the Oilers to rest Fuhr and keep both goaltenders sharp for the playoffs.

The 1987 playoffs were marked by several gruelling series, none more so than the Stanley Cup Final against the Philadelphia Flyers. The Flyers, seeking revenge for their loss two years earlier, pushed the Oilers to the brink in a seven-game series still regarded as one of the greatest Finals in NHL history. The series was a test of endurance, skill, and mental toughness, with both teams delivering memorable performances.

Moog's contributions were critical during the series, particularly in games where Fuhr needed relief or support. His ability to step into high-pressure situations and deliver strong performances was key to the Oilers' success. The final game of the series, held at the Northlands Coliseum in Edmonton, was a tense affair. The Oilers won 3-1, with Moog playing a crucial role in helping to secure the victory. The win gave the Oilers their third Stanley Cup in four years, cementing their legacy as one of the greatest teams in NHL history.

Throughout these three championship runs, Moog's role was defined by his consistency, reliability, and ability to perform under pressure. He was not just a backup goaltender but a vital part of the Oilers' dynasty, providing the team with the depth and security needed to compete at the highest level. Moog's contributions were often behind the scenes, but they were no less important than those of the team's more celebrated stars.

Moog's performance in these three Stanley Cup victories showcased his importance to the Oilers' success. His ability to handle the most intense moments of the playoffs and his steady presence in the net made him a key figure in one of the most dominant teams in hockey history. Moog's legacy is forever tied to the Oilers' dynasty, and his role in their championship successes is a testament to his skill, professionalism, and dedication to the game.

Moog's Key Performances in Crucial Playoff Games

Andy Moog's career is a tapestry of crucial playoff performances demonstrating his resilience, talent, and ability to shine in the most pressure-filled moments. As a goaltender, Moog's contributions in these high-stakes situations were instrumental in the success of the teams he played for, and his performances in the postseason often solidified his reputation as a reliable and clutch player.

One of the most memorable aspects of Moog's playoff career was his role in the Edmonton Oilers' success during the 1980s. Even though Grant Fuhr was often the starter, Moog consistently performed stellarly when called upon. His ability to step into the net and deliver under pressure was a significant asset for the Oilers, especially during their multiple Stanley Cup runs.

In the 1984 playoffs, Moog's performance was particularly noteworthy during the Smythe Division Finals against the Calgary Flames. The series was fiercely competitive, with both teams battling for supremacy. When Fuhr could not play due to injury, Moog was thrust into the spotlight. Despite the intense pressure, Moog performed admirably, making critical saves that helped the Oilers advance to the Stanley Cup Final. His composure and quick reflexes were fully displayed, proving he could be relied upon in the most challenging circumstances.

Another key performance came during the 1987 Stanley Cup Finals against the Philadelphia Flyers. The series was a gruelling seven-game battle that pushed both teams to their limits. Moog's role was vital during this series, particularly in games where Fuhr needed rest or when the team needed a change in momentum. In one of the games, Moog was called upon to relieve Fuhr and managed to maintain the team's composure, making crucial saves that kept the Oilers in the game. His calm and focused demeanour in these high-pressure situations allowed the Oilers to continue their aggressive style of play, knowing they had a solid presence in the net.

Moog's ability to perform in crucial playoff games was not limited to his time with the Oilers. After being traded to the Boston Bruins, Moog continued to demonstrate his playoff prowess. One of the standout moments in his Bruins career came during the 1988 Stanley Cup playoffs. The Bruins were up against the New Jersey Devils in the Wales Conference Finals, a series that tested their resolve and determination. Moog's performance was spectacular, particularly in Game 6, where he made several key saves that preserved the Bruins' lead and secured their spot in the Stanley Cup Finals. His ability to rise to the occasion in such a pivotal game underscored his value as a clutch performer.

In the 1990 playoffs, Moog again proved his mettle during the Bruins' run to the Stanley Cup Final. The Bruins faced the Washington Capitals in the Wales Conference Finals, and Moog's goaltending was a significant factor in the team's success. In Game 7, with the series on the line, Moog delivered one of his most memorable playoff performances. He stood tall in the net, ignoring numerous high-quality scoring chances from the Capitals. His poise under pressure and ability to make critical saves at key moments were crucial in the Bruins' victory, propelling them to the Final against the Edmonton Oilers.

Moog's time with the Dallas Stars also saw him deliver crucial playoff performances, particularly during the 1994 playoffs. The Stars were the underdogs heading into their series against the St. Louis Blues in the first round. Moog's goaltending was the key to the Stars' upset victory, especially in Game 7, where he was outstanding. He made several game-saving stops that kept the Stars in the contest, and his leadership and experience were evident as he guided the team to a hard-fought win. Moog's performance in that series reminded him of his ability to elevate his game when it mattered most.

Throughout his career, Moog's performances in crucial playoff games were characterized by his mental toughness, agility, and unwavering focus. His ability to perform under pressure was a hallmark of his playoff success, and it earned him the respect of teammates, coaches, and opponents alike. Whether he was playing as a starter or stepping in as a backup, Moog's playoff performances were often the difference between victory and defeat for his teams.

Moog's playoff legacy is also defined by his consistency across multiple teams and playoff runs. His adaptability and ability to quickly adjust to the demands of playoff hockey made him an invaluable asset throughout his career. Whether facing breakaways, power plays, or intense offensive pressure, Moog consistently delivered when his team needed him most.

The 1995 playoffs were another highlight of Moog's postseason career, this time with the Dallas Stars. The Stars faced the Detroit Red Wings in the first round, a series where the Red Wings were heavily favoured. Moog's goaltending was exceptional throughout the series, particularly in Game 5, where he faced a barrage of shots from the Red Wings' potent offence. Despite the overwhelming pressure, Moog made numerous acrobatic saves that kept the Stars in the game. His performance in that series, though the Stars were eventually eliminated, was a testament to his enduring skill and competitive spirit.

Moog's ability to perform in high-stakes situations also extended to his international career. During the 1988 Winter Olympics in Calgary, Moog represented Team Canada, and his goaltending was pivotal in several key games. His experience and composure were invaluable to the team, particularly during the medal round, where every game was critical. Moog's performances on the international stage added another layer to his legacy as a clutch playoff performer, capable of delivering for his country on the world's biggest stage.

Throughout his career, Moog's playoff performances were marked by his resilience, ability to remain calm under pressure, and his knack for making the crucial save when needed most. His playoff success across different teams and eras of his career speaks to his versatility and deep understanding of the game. Moog's legacy as a goaltender is inextricably linked to his ability to perform in the playoffs, where he consistently proved that he was not just a good goaltender but a great one who could be counted on when everything was on the line.

Relationship and Rivalry with Grant Fuhr as a Dynamic Goaltending Duo

Andy Moog's relationship with Grant Fuhr during their time together on the Edmonton Oilers is one of NHL history's most intriguing and dynamic chapters. The two goaltenders formed a tandem that contributed to the Oilers' dominance in the 1980s and reshaped how teams approached the goaltending position. The balance between their competitive rivalry and mutual respect was crucial in creating a partnership that became the backbone of the team's success.

When Moog joined the Oilers, Grant Fuhr was already establishing himself as one of the top young goaltenders in the league. Fuhr, known for his athleticism and ability to make spectacular saves, was the Oilers' primary netminder. Moog, drafted by the Oilers in 1980, quickly made a name for himself as a capable and reliable goaltender. From the outset, the two goaltenders were placed in a situation that could have easily bred hate, but instead, it led to a unique partnership built on a shared goal of winning.

The competition between Moog and Fuhr was intense, as both were determined to be the number one goaltender. They were two very different players in terms of style and temperament. Yet, their contrasting approaches to the game complemented each other and provided the Oilers with a versatile and formidable goaltending duo. Fuhr was known for his quick reflexes, incredible glove hand, and ability to perform acrobatic saves, while Moog was more methodical, relying on positioning, consistency, and mental toughness.

Despite the natural rivalry, Moog and Fuhr developed a working relationship marked by mutual respect. They understood that their competition was not personal but a driving force that improved each of them. The presence of another elite goaltender pushed both to elevate their games, knowing that any lapse could result in the other taking over the starting role. This internal competition kept both goaltenders sharp and focused, which was crucial for a team with championship aspirations.

The Oilers' coaching staff, led by Glen Sather, recognized the value of having two high-calibre goaltenders and often rotated them based on performance and matchups. While uncommon at the time, this rotation system proved effective as it allowed both Moog and Fuhr to stay fresh and maintain their competitive edge throughout the gruelling NHL season and playoffs. The strategy also provided the team with a safety net, ensuring that if one goaltender struggled or was injured, the other could step in seamlessly without a drop in performance.

One of the defining moments of their partnership came during the 1984 Stanley Cup playoffs. Fuhr was the starting goaltender, but an injury in the Smythe Division Finals against the Calgary Flames forced him out of the lineup. Patiently waiting for his opportunity, Moog stepped into the spotlight and delivered a series of clutch performances that helped the Oilers advance to the Stanley Cup Finals. His ability to rise to the occasion under immense pressure was a testament to his readiness and the competitive environment fostered between him and Fuhr.

The success of the Moog-Fuhr tandem was not without its challenges. The desire to be the starter meant that both goaltenders had to navigate the psychological aspect of sharing the net, which could easily strain relationships. However, Moog and Fuhr managed to maintain a professional relationship throughout their time together, largely because they both prioritized the team's success over personal accolades. Their ability to coexist and thrive as a duo reflected their maturity and understanding of their roles within the team.

Their different personalities also characterized Moog and Fuhr's rivalry. Fuhr was known for his laid-back demeanour, rarely showing signs of stress or pressure. His playing style reflected this calmness, where he often made difficult saves look easy. On the other hand, Moog was more intense and cerebral in his approach to the game. He meticulously prepared for each match, studying opponents and focusing on his mental preparation. These differing approaches added another layer to their relationship, as they often learned from each other, incorporating elements of each other's style into their games.

Off the ice, Moog and Fuhr were not close friends, but they shared a mutual respect crucial to their professional relationship. They recognized that their rivalry was beneficial for themselves and the entire team. The presence of two elite goaltenders created a competitive environment that kept both of them at the top of their game. It also allowed the Oilers to deploy a dual-threat in net, which was especially valuable during the long and arduous playoff runs.

Their relationship evolved as they each experienced personal and professional milestones. Moog eventually sought an opportunity to be a full-time starter, which led to his departure from the Oilers in 1987 when he was traded to the Boston Bruins. This move allowed Moog to step out of Fuhr's shadow and establish himself as a leading goaltender in his own right. Despite the separation, the legacy of their time together in Edmonton remained a significant part of both players' careers.

Reflecting on their time together, Moog and Fuhr's dynamic as a goaltending duo has often been cited as one of the best in NHL history. Their ability to balance rivalry with teamwork set a precedent for how goaltending tandems could operate in a league traditionally relying on a single starting goaltender. The respect and professionalism they exhibited contributed to the Oilers' success and earned them both places in hockey history.

Moog's departure from Edmonton did not diminish his respect for Fuhr, nor did it change how he viewed their time as teammates. In interviews and retrospectives, Moog has spoken fondly of their rivalry, acknowledging that Fuhr's presence pushed him to improve and that their competition was a crucial part of the Oilers' dynasty. Fuhr, too, has recognized Moog's contributions and the importance of their partnership during those championship years.

The Moog-Fuhr tandem remains a quintessential example of how competition can coexist with collaboration and how two athletes competing for the same position can drive each other to greatness. Their relationship, marked by rivalry and respect, was a key component of the Edmonton Oilers' success during one of the most dominant eras in NHL history. Their legacy continues to influence how teams manage goaltending duos, proving that teamwork and mutual respect can lead to extraordinary success even in a position traditionally dominated by individual play.

Chapter 4: A New Chapter in Boston

The Trade to the Boston Bruins in 1988 and the Shift to Becoming a Starting Goaltender

The trade to the Boston Bruins in 1988 marked a significant turning point in Andy Moog's career, transforming him from a reliable backup goaltender into a primary starter and solidifying his place as one of the elite goaltenders in the NHL. This move allowed Moog to step out of the shadow of Grant Fuhr, his counterpart in Edmonton and fully showcase his abilities on a grander stage in a city hungry for hockey success.

By the time Moog was traded to Boston, he had already established himself as a dependable and skilled goaltender with the Edmonton Oilers. Despite being part of one of the most successful teams in NHL history, Moog often found himself in the backup role due to the presence of Fuhr, who was widely regarded as one of the best goaltenders of the era. While Moog played a crucial role in several of the Oilers' playoff runs, including their Stanley Cup victories, he yearned for a position where he could be the definitive starter and lead a team in his own right.

The trade came at a time of change and restructuring for the Oilers. Moog had expressed dissatisfaction with his backup role and desire for a more prominent position on the ice. The Bruins, on the other hand, needed a reliable goaltender who could provide stability and consistency in the net. The deal was mutually beneficial: the Oilers received left winger Geoff Courtnall, while the Bruins acquired a goaltender eager to prove himself as a top starter in the league.

Upon his arrival in Boston, Moog was immediately thrust into the spotlight. The Bruins, a storied franchise with a passionate fan base, were trying to reclaim their position as one of the NHL's elite teams. Boston's goaltending situation had been inconsistent, and there was a clear need for a goaltender who could bring skill and leadership to the crease. Moog's arrival was seen as a key piece in the puzzle, giving the team a sense of confidence and security that had been lacking.

Stepping into the starting role for the Bruins was a challenge that Moog embraced wholeheartedly. He brought the experience of being part of a dynasty in Edmonton, along with a work ethic and professionalism that quickly earned him the respect of his new teammates. Moog's technical proficiency and calm demeanour under pressure were assets the Bruins desperately needed. He became a stabilizing force on the ice, providing the team with the reliable goaltending essential for sustained success in the NHL.

Moog's impact on the Bruins was felt almost immediately. In his first season with Boston, he played a pivotal role in leading the team to the playoffs. His consistent performance and ability to make key saves in critical moments helped the Bruins advance to the Stanley Cup Finals in 1988, just months after his arrival. Although the Edmonton Oilers ultimately defeated the Bruins in the Finals, Moog's performance throughout the playoffs solidified his status as a top-tier goaltender.

The trade to Boston allowed Moog to redefine his career, transitioning from a player often seen as a reliable second option to a goaltender who could be counted on as the backbone of a team. His success with the Bruins was not limited to his first season; Moog became a key figure for the team throughout the late 1980s and early 1990s. His consistency in net, combined with his experience and leadership, made him an integral part of the Bruins' success during that period.

Moog's relationship with the Bruins organization and fan base grew stronger with each passing season. Boston, known for its passionate sports culture, embraced Moog as one of their own. His work ethic and dedication to the team resonated with the fans, who appreciated his steady presence in the net. Moog's ability to handle the pressure of playing in a city like Boston, where expectations are always high, further endeared him to the fan base.

During his time with the Bruins, Moog faced the challenge of maintaining his performance while dealing with the physical and mental demands of being a starting goaltender in the NHL. Unlike his time in Edmonton, where he often shared duties with Fuhr, Moog was now the clear number-one goaltender for the Bruins. This role came with increased responsibilities, including handling most of the team's games and being the go-to player in critical situations. Moog met these challenges head-on, demonstrating his resilience and ability to perform at a high level over an extended period.

One of the defining aspects of Moog's tenure with the Bruins was his ability to elevate his game during the playoffs. Known for his clutch performances, Moog was often at his best when the stakes were highest. His playoff heroics included several memorable series, where his goaltending was a key factor in the Bruins' success. Whether it was making a game-saving stop in overtime or outdueling an opposing goaltender in a low-scoring contest, Moog's playoff performances were a testament to his mental toughness and skill.

Moog's transition to becoming a starting goaltender in Boston also highlighted his adaptability as a player. Throughout his career, Moog has demonstrated the ability to adjust to different roles and situations. In Boston, he was asked to take on the role of a leader, not just in terms of his play on the ice but also in the locker room. Moog's calm and composed demeanour made him a natural leader, someone his teammates could rely on during both good times and bad. His experience in Edmonton was invaluable, as he brought a championship mentality to a team striving to reach that level.

Over the years, Moog's time in Boston cemented his legacy as one of the great goaltenders of his era. He became synonymous with consistency and excellence in the net, qualities every team seeks in a starting goaltender. His trade to the Bruins not only allowed him to shine as a starter but also allowed him to leave an indelible mark on the franchise. Moog's contributions to the Bruins during this period were significant, helping to reestablish the team as a perennial contender and earning him a place in the hearts of Boston fans.

The shift to becoming a starting goaltender in Boston also represented a personal triumph for Moog. After years of being a part of a goaltending tandem in Edmonton, he could fully embrace the role of a number-one goaltender. This transition was not without its challenges, but Moog's success in Boston proved that he could handle the pressures and responsibilities that came with the position. His ability to thrive in this role was a testament to his talent, work ethic, and determination.

Moog's trade to the Boston Bruins in 1988 was a turning point that allowed him to showcase his skills on a larger stage, transitioning from a backup to a star. His time with the Bruins highlighted his consistency, leadership, and ability to perform under pressure, solidifying his status as one of the top goaltenders of his generation.

Immediate Impact on the Bruins' Performance and Leading them to the Stanley Cup Finals

When Andy Moog joined the Boston Bruins in 1988, the team was looking to reclaim its position as one of the dominant forces in the NHL. The Bruins, steeped in hockey tradition, had a storied past, but the late 1980s had seen the team struggle to break through in the playoffs. With Moog in the net, the team gained a talented goaltender and a leader who had been part of multiple championship-winning teams with the Edmonton Oilers. His arrival marked a turning point for the Bruins, eager to make a deep playoff run and possibly secure the Stanley Cup.

Moog's impact on the Bruins was almost immediate. His experience, poise under pressure, and technical skills gave the team a new confidence level. The Bruins' defence, which had been solid but occasionally inconsistent, found stability with Moog as their last line of defence. His calm demeanour in the crease was infectious, spreading throughout the roster and allowing the Bruins to play with a level of assurance that had been missing in previous seasons. Moog's presence gave the team the belief that they could compete with the best in the league.

From the moment he put on the Bruins' jersey, Moog began to deliver the kind of performances that would solidify his reputation as one of the premier goaltenders in the NHL. During the regular season, Moog consistently turned in strong outings, providing the team with reliable goaltending night after night. His ability to read plays, anticipate the opposition's moves, and make clutch saves at critical moments helped the Bruins secure a spot in the playoffs. The team responded to Moog's steady play by rallying around him, knowing they had a goaltender capable of stealing games when needed.

Moog's role became even more critical as the Bruins entered the playoffs. The postseason is where legends are made, and Moog was determined to add to his already impressive resume. He elevated his game as the stakes grew, displaying a concentration and focus that allowed him to thrive in the intense environment of playoff hockey. Moog's calmness in the net, even in the most chaotic situations, gave the Bruins the backbone they needed to push through each round.

The Bruins' path to the Stanley Cup Finals was anything but easy. They faced tough competition from teams that were just as hungry for success. However, Moog's goaltending was key to the Bruins' ability to advance through the playoff rounds. In each series, Moog was called upon to make critical saves, often in tight, low-scoring games where one mistake could mean the difference between winning and losing. His ability to rise to the occasion during these high-pressure moments was one of the defining features of his playoff run with the Bruins.

One of the most memorable aspects of Moog's impact during the Bruins' playoff journey was his consistency. Night after night, he delivered performances that kept the Bruins in games, giving them a chance to win even when the opposition outplayed them. Moog's experience in previous playoff battles with the Oilers had prepared him for the grind of the postseason, and he brought that knowledge to the Bruins, helping to guide a team that was eager to prove itself. As the Bruins advanced to the Stanley Cup Finals, Moog's leadership became increasingly evident. He was not just a goaltender; he was a stabilizing force and a mentor for many of the younger players on the team. Moog's experience in winning championships with the Oilers allowed him to provide invaluable guidance to his teammates, many of whom were experiencing the intensity of the Finals for the first time. His calm, measured approach to the game helped keep the team focused on the task, even as the pressure mounted with each passing game.

The 1988 Stanley Cup Finals saw the Bruins face off against the Edmonton Oilers, Moog's former team. This matchup added an extra layer of drama to the series, as Moog was now tasked with stopping the very team that he had helped to win three Stanley Cups. The Oilers were an offensive juggernaut, boasting some of the greatest players in NHL history, including Wayne Gretzky and Mark Messier. Moog's familiarity with the Oilers' style of play gave the Bruins an edge, as he knew the tendencies and habits of many of the Oilers' stars.

Moog's performances during the Finals were a testament to his skill and mental toughness. Despite facing one of the most potent offences in NHL history, Moog stood tall in net, making save after save to keep the Bruins in the series. His ability to remain composed under relentless pressure was remarkable, and it allowed the Bruins to compete against the Oilers, who were heavily favoured to win the series. Moog's goaltending was the key factor in Boston's ability to extend the series and challenge the Oilers in ways few teams managed to do.

Although the Bruins did not ultimately win the Stanley Cup, falling to the Oilers in the Finals, Moog's impact on the team's performance was undeniable. His goaltending was the cornerstone of the Bruins' playoff run, and his ability to perform at such a high level on the biggest stage earned him widespread respect and admiration. Moog had proven that he was capable of being a starting goaltender and a leader who could carry a team deep into the playoffs.

Moog's immediate impact on the Bruins went beyond just his on-ice performance. He brought a winning mentality to a team striving to return to its former glory. The Bruins, inspired by Moog's play, adopted a more determined and resilient attitude, which became a hallmark of the team in the years that followed. Moog's influence was felt not just in the crease but throughout the entire organization, as his professionalism and work ethic set a standard for others to follow.

The 1988 playoff run, highlighted by Moog's stellar goaltending, marked the beginning of a new era for the Boston Bruins. With Moog as their starting goaltender, the Bruins knew they had a chance to compete for the Stanley Cup every year. His impact on the team's performance during that first season set the stage for future successes as the Bruins continued to build around their star goaltender.

Moog's legacy with the Bruins was cemented by his ability to step into the starting role and immediately lead the team to the Stanley Cup Finals. His arrival in Boston revitalized the franchise and gave the team the goaltending stability it sought. Moog's immediate impact was a key factor in the Bruins' return to prominence in the NHL, and his contributions during the 1988 playoffs remain a defining chapter in his storied career.

Memorable Moments and Standout Performances during His Time in Boston

During Andy Moog's tenure with the Boston Bruins, he delivered a series of performances that solidified his reputation as one of his era's most reliable and resilient goaltenders. These moments were not just significant in the context of single games but often turned the tide of entire series or seasons, leaving a lasting impact on the team and its fans. Moog's time with the Bruins was marked by a blend of spectacular saves, unwavering consistency, and a knack for rising to the occasion in the most critical moments.

One of Moog's most memorable performances came during the 1990 Stanley Cup Playoffs. In a fiercely contested series, the Bruins faced the Montreal Canadiens, their long-time rivals. Game after game, the Canadiens pressured Moog with a relentless barrage of shots, but he stood tall, turning away nearly everything that came his way. In Game 5 of the series, Moog delivered one of his finest performances, making 33 saves in a thrilling overtime victory that gave the Bruins a crucial edge. His ability to remain composed under intense pressure was a testament to his experience and mental fortitude. That victory advanced the Bruins in the playoffs and added another chapter to the storied rivalry between Boston and Montreal, with Moog playing the hero's role.

Another standout moment in Moog's career with the Bruins occurred during the 1991 Eastern Conference Finals against the Pittsburgh Penguins. The Penguins, led by stars like Mario Lemieux and Jaromir Jagr, boasted one of the most potent offences in the league. Despite the overwhelming firepower of the Penguins, Moog was determined to give his team a fighting chance. In Game 2 of the series, Moog delivered a performance for the ages, stopping 35 shots and allowing the Bruins to steal a game on the road. His reflexes and anticipation were fully displayed as he repeatedly denied Lemieux and Jagr from close range. Although the Bruins would eventually fall to the Penguins in the series, Moog's effort in Game 2 stood out as a shining example of his ability to elevate his game when it mattered most.

The regular season also provided Moog with numerous opportunities to showcase his skills. One particularly memorable game occurred on January 3, 1992, against the New York Rangers. The Bruins were amid a tough stretch, and the Rangers, led by Mark Messier, were one of the top teams in the league. Moog was sensational that night, making 40 saves in a 3-0 shutout victory. His performance was a masterclass in goaltending, as he controlled rebounds, made acrobatic saves, and frustrated the Rangers' shooters at every turn. The shutout was Moog's 19th of his career and one of the most impressive, given the quality of the opposition. That game reminded the league that Moog could single-handedly win games for his team, even against the best of the best.

Another unforgettable moment came during the 1993 Stanley Cup Playoffs in a first-round series against the Buffalo Sabres. The series was a hard-fought battle, with both teams exchanging victories and no clear favourite emerging. In Game 6, with the Bruins facing elimination, Moog delivered a stunning 36-save performance to force a decisive Game 7. His poise and technical precision were fully displayed, particularly during a tense third period where the Sabres pressed for the equalizer. Moog's ability to stay cool under pressure and timely saves kept the Bruins' hopes alive. In Game 7, Moog was again the backbone of the team, stopping 28 shots and leading the Bruins to a series-clinching victory. His back-to-back stellar performances in Games 6 and 7 were a testament to his status as one of the best playoff goaltenders of his time.

Moog's time with the Bruins was also marked by his consistent play against the elite teams of the NHL. Whether facing the powerhouse Edmonton Oilers, the dynamic Penguins, or the rival Canadiens, Moog saved his best performances for the toughest opponents. His ability to rise to the occasion in these high-stakes games endeared him to Bruins fans and earned him respect throughout the league.

Moog's consistency in delivering standout performances during key matchups was one of the hallmarks of his career in Boston, and it was this ability that made him one of the most reliable goaltenders in the league.

Beyond individual games, Moog's presence in the Bruins' lineup brought stability to a team that had often struggled with goaltending consistency before his arrival. His ability to string together stretches of dominant play was crucial during long regular seasons and deep playoff runs. Moog's resilience and mental toughness were particularly evident during the grind of the playoffs, where he consistently provided the Bruins with the goaltending needed to compete for the Stanley Cup. His ability to maintain a high level of play over multiple playoff rounds was one of the reasons the Bruins were perennial contenders during his time with the team.

Moog's relationship with the Boston fans also added to the memorability of his time with the Bruins. Known for his calm demeanour and workmanlike approach to the game, Moog became a fan favourite, respected for his play on the ice and his character off it. He was seen as a player who embodied the values of hard work, dedication, and humility, qualities that resonated deeply with the passionate Boston fanbase. Moog's performances in clutch moments and his approachable personality made him one of the most beloved players in the city.

One of the most touching moments of Moog's career in Boston came during his final home game with the Bruins in 1993. As the final buzzer sounded, signalling a Bruins victory, the crowd at the Boston Garden erupted in a prolonged standing ovation for Moog, recognizing his contributions to the team over the years. Moog, ever the consummate professional, acknowledged the fans with a wave, but the moment's emotion was clear. It was a fitting tribute to a player who had given so much to the team and the city during his time with the Bruins.

Moog's standout performances during his years with the Bruins were characterized by his ability to deliver under pressure, consistency across seasons, and ability to inspire his teammates and fans. Whether it was in a crucial playoff game, a regular-season battle against a top opponent, or an emotional farewell, Moog always seemed to find a way to rise to the occasion. His time in Boston was marked by memorable moments that not only defined his career but also left an indelible mark on the history of the Bruins.

The Challenge of Facing His Former Team, the Oilers, in the 1990 Stanley Cup Finals

The 1990 Stanley Cup Finals presented a unique and emotionally charged challenge for Andy Moog. Having spent several seasons with the Edmonton Oilers, where he played a pivotal role in their success during the 1980s, Moog found himself on the opposite side of the ice, now the starting goaltender for the Boston Bruins. Facing his former team in the Finals was not just a test of his physical skills but also an examination of his mental fortitude and emotional resilience. The series would bring Moog face-to-face with many former teammates, players with whom he had shared the glory of three Stanley Cup victories. The task was immense: leading the Bruins to their first championship since 1972 by defeating the team that had been the dominant force in the NHL throughout the decade. From the outset, the 1990 Finals carried an intense emotional weight for Moog. His departure from Edmonton had been amicable, but leaving a team that had been such a significant part of his life was still difficult. The Oilers had been his first NHL home, where he had developed from a young goaltender into a Stanley Cup champion. Now, as the Bruins' number one goaltender, Moog had to put aside any sentimental feelings and focus entirely on the task at hand. The series was not just another set of games; it was a battle against the team that had once been his family.

Game 1 of the series was held in Boston, and the anticipation was palpable. Moog knew that his performance would be under intense scrutiny, not only because of the stakes of the Finals but also because of the personal history he shared with the Oilers. The opening game was a tightly contested affair, with both teams displaying the skill and determination that had brought them to this stage. Moog was solid between the pipes, making several key saves to keep the game close. However, the Oilers, led by Mark Messier and Jari Kurri, managed to edge out an overtime victory, winning 3-2. Despite the loss, Moog's performance was commendable, and he remained focused on the bigger picture. The series was far from over, and Moog knew that his experience and leadership would be crucial as the Bruins looked to bounce back.

The pressure on Moog intensified as the series moved to Edmonton for Game 3. Returning to Northlands Coliseum, where he had once been cheered by thousands of Oilers fans, was a surreal experience. Now, as the enemy in the eyes of the Edmonton faithful, Moog was greeted with a chorus of boos whenever he made a save or touched the puck. The emotional weight of playing in his former home was immense, but Moog used it as fuel to elevate his game. He knew that to have any chance of securing the Stanley Cup, he would need to be at his best.

Game 3 was a critical juncture in the series, and Moog delivered one of his finest performances. He made 29 saves, including several spectacular stops in the third period, to help the Bruins secure a 2-1 victory and pull within a game of the Oilers. Moog's poise under pressure was evident throughout the contest, as he remained calm and composed despite the hostile environment. His ability to block out the noise and focus on the task was a testament to his experience and mental toughness. The victory gave the Bruins new life in the series and reinforced the belief that they could compete with the Oilers, even in their building.

However, the Oilers responded in Game 4 with a dominant performance, shutting out the Bruins 5-0. Despite the loss, Moog remained resilient, understanding that setbacks were part of the journey. The series shifted back to Boston for Game 5, with the Bruins facing elimination. Moog's leadership was critical during this time, as he provided a steadying presence in the locker room and on the ice. He knew his teammates would look to him for inspiration and that his play would set the tone for the entire team.

Game 5 was a battle of wills, with both teams desperate to control the game's tempo. Moog was exceptional, turning aside shot after shot and giving the Bruins a chance to extend the series. The game remained tied late into the third period, but the Oilers' relentless pressure eventually broke through, and they scored the game-winning goal with just over two minutes remaining. The Bruins' season came to a heartbreaking end, and Moog was left to reflect on what could have been.

For Moog, the 1990 Stanley Cup Finals were a bittersweet experience. On one hand, he had proven himself as a top-tier goaltender, capable of leading a team to the brink of a championship. On the other, he had fallen short against a team that he knew so well, a team that had been a significant part of his journey. The series was a reminder of the fine line between victory and defeat in the NHL, where the smallest margins can determine the outcome of a season. The emotional toll of the series was undeniable, but it also catalyzed Moog's continued growth as a player. He had faced the ultimate challenge of competing against his former team on the grandest stage and had done so with dignity and professionalism. The experience strengthened his resolve and deepened his understanding of what it took to succeed at the sport's highest level.

In the aftermath of the series, Moog's reputation as a clutch performer was further solidified. His ability to handle the pressure of the Finals, particularly against a team with such personal significance, earned him widespread respect throughout the league.

While the Bruins did not capture the Stanley Cup that year, Moog's performance was a major reason they had made it to the Finals in the first place. He had given them a chance to compete, and his leadership, both on and off the ice, was invaluable.

The 1990 Finals also marked a turning point in Moog's career, reinforcing his status as a starting goaltender who could lead a team deep into the playoffs. The lessons he learned from facing his former team would stay with him throughout the rest of his career, shaping how he approached the game and prepared for high-stakes situations.

For the Oilers, defeating Moog and the Bruins was a significant achievement, but they, too, recognized the challenge he had presented. Many of his former teammates spoke highly of Moog after the series, acknowledging the difficulty of facing a goaltender who knew their tendencies so well. The mutual respect between Moog and the Oilers was evident, adding complexity to the rivalry that had developed during the series.

The 1990 Stanley Cup Finals were a defining moment in Andy Moog's career, a test of character, skill, and perseverance. Facing his former team in such a high-pressure situation was a challenge unlike any he had faced before, but Moog rose to the occasion, demonstrating why he was one of the most respected goaltenders in the NHL. The series was a testament to his abilities and a reminder of the deep connections within the hockey world, where former teammates can quickly become fierce competitors.

Chapter 5: Consistency in Dallas

Moog's Move to the Dallas Stars and His Role as a Veteran Leader

In 1992, Andy Moog transitioned to a new chapter in his career when he joined the Dallas Stars. This move marked a significant shift for Moog, who had spent most of his NHL career with the Edmonton Oilers and the Boston Bruins. The Stars, a relatively young franchise that had recently relocated from Minnesota, were eager to make their mark in the NHL, and Moog's arrival was seen as a crucial step in that process.

The decision to sign with the Dallas Stars came when the team built a competitive roster. The Stars were looking for stability in goal and experienced leadership to guide their young players through the challenges of the NHL. Moog's reputation as a seasoned goaltender with a proven track record made him an ideal candidate for the veteran mentor role. His experience, especially his success with the Oilers and Bruins, was invaluable for a team still finding its identity.

From the moment Moog arrived in Dallas, it was clear that he was more than just a player; he was a leader on and off the ice. His presence brought a sense of professionalism and confidence to the Stars' locker room. Young players like Ed Belfour, who would go on to become a star in his own right, looked up to Moog not only for his on-ice skills but also for his approach to the game. Moog's work ethic, dedication, and calm demeanour inspired his teammates and set a standard for the team.

During his time with the Stars, Moog's role was multifaceted. He was tasked with stabilizing the goaltending position, which had been inconsistent for the team. His arrival provided a solid and reliable option between the pipes, giving the Stars a better chance to compete in games and make a push for the playoffs. Moog's technical skill and experience helped improve the team's overall defensive play, and his ability to handle pressure was particularly beneficial during crucial moments in the season.

One of the defining aspects of Moog's time with the Stars was his role as a mentor. The young players on the team benefited greatly from his guidance. Moog took on a coaching-like role, sharing insights and offering advice to his less experienced teammates. He worked closely with the team's younger goaltenders, helping them refine their techniques and understand the nuances of playing in the NHL. His mentorship extended beyond just the technical aspects of goaltending; he also imparted lessons about handling the mental and emotional challenges of being a professional athlete.

Moog's influence was felt in the locker room as well. His leadership style was characterized by quiet strength and respect. He led by example, demonstrating the importance of preparation, focus, and perseverance. Moog's ability to remain composed and confident, even in high-pressure situations, served as a stabilizing force for the entire team. His presence helped foster a positive team environment where younger players felt supported and motivated to perform at their best.

On the ice, Moog continued to showcase the skills that had made him a successful goaltender throughout his career. He gave the Stars consistent and reliable performances, often making crucial saves in key moments. His experience handling high-stress situations was evident, and he played a significant role in helping the Stars remain competitive in their games. Moog's contributions were not always reflected in the statistics, but his impact on the team's overall performance and morale was substantial.

During the 1992-93 season, Moog's leadership and experience were instrumental in guiding the Stars to the playoffs. Under his guidance, the team showed significant improvement from previous years, demonstrating that adding a veteran goaltender could have a transformative effect. Moog's ability to perform at a high level, combined with his mentorship, was a key factor in the Stars' success.

Moog's role became even more critical as the team progressed through the playoffs. The pressure of postseason hockey required a goaltender who could remain focused and perform under intense scrutiny. Moog's ability to stay calm and collected during these high-pressure games was valuable. He provided the Stars with stability and confidence, knowing they had a goaltender with a proven track record in big games.

Moog's impact on the Stars was not limited to his playing career. After his time with the team, he remained involved in hockey and contributed to the sport in various ways. His experience and insights were sought after by teams and players alike, and he remained a respected figure in the hockey community. Moog's move to the Dallas Stars was a significant milestone in his career, marking the beginning of a new chapter that allowed him to share his knowledge and experience with a new generation of players.

In retrospect, Moog's time with the Stars was a testament to his enduring talent and leadership. His ability to adapt to a new team and take on a mentor role demonstrated his versatility and commitment to the game. Moog's legacy as a goaltender and leader extended beyond his years with the Oilers and Bruins, leaving a lasting impact on the Dallas Stars and their players. His contributions to the team were measured in victories and saves and in the positive influence he had on the development of the next generation of hockey talent.

The Importance of His Stability and Experience in a Young, Developing Team

In the early 1990s, the Dallas Stars were in a period of transition and growth, striving to establish themselves in the NHL after relocating from Minnesota. For a young team like the Stars, integrating a seasoned veteran like Andy Moog into their roster proved to be a crucial move. His presence provided more than just a reliable goaltender; it offered a stabilizing influence essential for a franchise navigating its developmental phase.

The Dallas Stars were a team in the midst of building their identity. They had a mix of emerging talent and players still finding their footing in the NHL. Having a goaltender with Moog's extensive experience and proven track record was invaluable in such a context. His ability to deliver consistent performances between the pipes brought a sense of reliability to the team, which was crucial for instilling confidence within the locker room and among the coaching staff.

One of the key benefits of Moog's presence was his role in providing stability. A young team often faces challenges in maintaining consistent performance, and goaltending is a critical area where inconsistency can be particularly damaging. By offering a steady hand in goal, Moog helped mitigate the impact of any fluctuations in team performance. His reliability meant that the team could count on him to perform at a high level regardless of the circumstances, which is a valuable asset for any developing squad.

Moog's experience also played a significant role in helping the Stars manage the pressures and challenges of the NHL. For many young players, the transition to the professional level can be overwhelming. The demands of the league, coupled with the expectations placed on them, can lead to stress and performance anxiety. Moog's calm demeanour and experience handling high-pressure situations were models for his teammates. His ability to stay composed during critical moments was a source of reassurance and helped alleviate some pressure on the younger players.

Another aspect of Moog's impact was his mentorship. Beyond his role on the ice, Moog became a guide for the younger team members. His insights into the game, drawn from years of experience with successful teams, offered valuable lessons on approaching various aspects of professional hockey. Moog could share practical knowledge about everything from game strategy to managing the mental and emotional aspects of being an NHL player. This mentorship helped accelerate the development of young talent by providing them with a clearer understanding of what it takes to succeed at the highest level.

Moog's leadership also extended to creating a positive team culture. Establishing a strong and supportive team environment is crucial for fostering growth and success in a developing team. Moog's professionalism and dedication set a standard for his teammates. His work ethic, approach to training, and attitude toward the game contributed to a culture of commitment and excellence. This culture was instrumental in helping the Stars build a foundation for future success, as it encouraged players to adopt similar values and strive for continuous improvement.

The impact of Moog's stability and experience was evident in regular-season performances and crucial games. During high-pressure situations, such as key games and playoff matches, Moog's ability to maintain a high level of play provided a sense of security for the team. Knowing they had a dependable goaltender helped the players focus on their roles and perform to the best of their abilities. Moog's performances in these critical moments underscored the importance of having a veteran presence in a young team's lineup.

Furthermore, Moog's time with the Stars highlighted the value of having an experienced player who could bridge the gap between the past and the future. As the team looked to build its legacy and establish itself as a competitive force, Moog's contributions helped pave the way for future successes. His ability to mentor young players while performing at a high level provided a blueprint for how experience and skill can complement each other to drive a team forward.

In retrospect, the role of Andy Moog in the Dallas Stars' development cannot be overstated. His stability, experience, and leadership were critical to the team's growth and success during his tenure. Moog's impact went beyond the immediate benefits of solid goaltending; he provided the team with a foundation of reliability and professionalism that contributed significantly to their long-term development. His influence on the young players and the overall team culture played a vital role in shaping the Stars into a more competitive and cohesive unit, setting the stage for future achievements in the NHL.

Contribution to the Stars' Rise as a Competitive Force in the NHL

Andy Moog's tenure with the Dallas Stars marked a transformative period for the franchise, during which he played a pivotal role in the team's evolution from an emerging squad into a competitive force in the NHL. His contributions went far beyond his role as a goaltender, impacting various facets of the team's development and success.

When Moog joined the Stars, the team was in a crucial phase of building its identity in the league. The Stars had recently relocated from Minnesota and were working to establish themselves in their new home in Dallas. In this context, Moog's presence provided a boost in goaltending and a significant influence on the team's overall progress.

One of the most significant ways Moog contributed was through his steady and reliable performance. His stability in goal was essential for a team still finding its footing. By consistently delivering solid performances, Moog allowed the Stars to build a strong defensive foundation. This reliability was critical for a team that needed to establish trust in its goaltender and gain confidence in its ability to compete at a high level.

Moog's experience was particularly valuable during the team's transition. The NHL can be a demanding and challenging environment, especially when a team is changing. Moog's extensive experience in the league helped him navigate the pressures of high-stakes games and the rigours of the NHL season. His ability to handle these challenges with composure and professionalism set a positive example for his teammates and contributed to a more resilient team culture.

Moreover, Moog's influence extended beyond the ice. His leadership in the locker room played a crucial role in shaping the team's culture. As a seasoned veteran, Moog brought professionalism and dedication that set a standard for the rest of the team. His work ethic, attitude toward training, and approach to the game were exemplary, helping to instil a culture of commitment and excellence within the organization.

Moog's mentorship was another key factor in the Stars' rise as a competitive force. Young players on the team benefited immensely from his guidance. Moog shared valuable insights into the nuances of professional hockey, offering advice on everything from game strategy to managing the mental aspects of the sport. His ability to mentor and support younger players helped accelerate their development and integration into the NHL, contributing to the team's overall improvement.

In addition to his on-ice contributions, Moog's impact was also felt in crucial moments of the season. During high-pressure games and pivotal matches, Moog's performance gave the team a sense of security. His ability to make critical saves and maintain a high level of play in important situations was a significant factor in the Stars' success. This reliability in clutch moments helped the team gain confidence and perform well under pressure.

Moog's time with the Stars also played a role in elevating the team's profile in the NHL. As the Stars began to show competitive potential, Moog's performances and leadership drew attention to the team's progress. The visibility and recognition gained through competitive play helped establish the Stars as a formidable opponent in the league. This newfound respect and recognition were important for the franchise's growth and development.

The synergy between Moog and his teammates was another element that contributed to the Stars' rise. His ability to integrate seamlessly with the team and build strong relationships with fellow players created a cohesive unit. This teamwork was crucial for the team's success, as it fostered a sense of unity and collective effort. Moog's presence helped enhance the overall team dynamics, leading to better performances.

Moog's contributions were evident in the team's improved performance and competitiveness. Under his influence, the Stars significantly improved their gameplay and results. The team's progression from an emerging squad to a competitive force in the NHL was a testament to Moog's role in their development. His steady goaltending, leadership, and mentorship were instrumental in helping the Stars reach new levels of success.

Andy Moog's time with the Dallas Stars was marked by his significant contributions to the team's rise as a competitive force in the NHL. His steady performance, leadership, and mentorship played crucial roles in shaping the team's development and success. Moog's impact extended beyond his on-ice achievements, influencing various aspects of the team's growth and establishing the Stars as a formidable presence in the league. His contributions left a lasting legacy on the franchise and played a key role in its evolution into a competitive NHL team.

Key Games and Moments that Solidified His Reputation in Dallas

Andy Moog's tenure with the Dallas Stars was marked by several key games and moments instrumental in solidifying his reputation as a pivotal figure in the team's history. These instances showcased his exceptional skills and highlighted his ability to perform under pressure, contributing significantly to the team's successes and enhancing his status as a cornerstone of the Stars' goaltending.

One of the defining moments of Moog's time with the Stars occurred during the 1989-1990 NHL season. The team, led by Moog's steady play in goal, demonstrated considerable progress. In a crucial matchup against the Calgary Flames, a formidable opponent, Moog's performance was a key factor in securing a vital victory. This game was significant for Moog as it highlighted his ability to deliver in high-pressure situations, a trait that became a hallmark of his career with Dallas. His strong showing against a top team helped cement his reputation as a reliable and skilled goaltender.

Another memorable moment came during the 1991-1992 NHL season when the Stars faced the Detroit Red Wings in a highly anticipated playoff series. The series tested the Stars' resilience and Moog's ability to rise to the occasion. In Game 4 of the series, Moog delivered an outstanding performance, making a series of crucial saves that kept the Stars in contention. His play was instrumental in the team's success, and his ability to stand tall in critical moments earned him praise and solidified his reputation as a clutch performer.

The 1993-1994 season was another highlight of Moog's tenure in Dallas. During this season, the Stars were vying for a strong position in the playoffs, and Moog's performances were pivotal in their push. In a particularly memorable game against the Chicago Blackhawks, Moog showcased his skills with a series of spectacular saves that secured a crucial win and demonstrated his ability to handle intense game situations. This game was a testament to Moog's consistency and his role as a reliable goaltender for the team.

One key game that stands out in Moog's Dallas career was a matchup against the Edmonton Oilers, his former team, in the 1993-1994 season. The game was significant not only because of the rivalry but also because of Moog's performance against his old teammates. In a game filled with emotion and high stakes, Moog made several crucial saves that played a major role in securing a victory for the Stars. This performance was a testament to his ability to rise above personal connections and focus on delivering for his new team, further solidifying his standing with the Stars.

Moog's leadership was also evident in the 1994-1995 season, which saw the Stars continue their competitive rise. In a key matchup against the Colorado Avalanche, Moog's experience and poise were on full display. The game was intense, with both teams vying for crucial points, and Moog's ability to keep his composure under pressure was instrumental in the Stars' success. His performance in this game clearly indicated his influence on the team's ability to perform in high-stress situations.

Another defining moment in Moog's career with the Stars was his role in the 1995-1996 season when the team made a strong playoff push. In a pivotal playoff game against the St. Louis Blues, Moog's play was a key factor in the Stars' victory. His performance in this game showcased his ability to maintain high-level play in crucial moments, further cementing his reputation as a reliable and skilled goaltender.

Moog's ability to contribute to the team's success was not limited to individual games but was also evident in his overall impact on the team's performance. Throughout his tenure with the Stars, he consistently demonstrated his skills and leadership, contributing to the team's growth and development. His performances in key games and his ability to deliver under pressure were instrumental in establishing the Stars as a competitive force in the NHL.

In the later years of Moog's career with the Stars, his consistent play and leadership continued to define his reputation. His ability to mentor younger players and his role in guiding the team through important games and moments were crucial in maintaining the team's competitive edge. Moog's legacy with the Stars was solidified by his outstanding performances and ability to significantly impact the team's success.

The key games and moments from Moog's time with the Dallas Stars played a crucial role in defining his career and establishing his reputation as one of the team's great goaltenders. His performances in high-pressure situations, leadership, and ability to contribute to the team's success were all integral to his legacy with the Stars. Moog's impact on the team was felt through his performances and overall influence on the team's growth and development.

Chapter 6: Closing Out With the Montreal Canadiens

The Final Phase of Moog's Playing Career with the Montreal Canadiens

As Andy Moog approached the final phase of his playing career, the Montreal Canadiens became the last team with which he would leave his mark on the NHL. By the time Moog joined the Canadiens, he was already an established and highly respected veteran goaltender known for his agility, composure under pressure, and ability to step up in crucial moments. Although relatively short, His tenure with Montreal was significant in rounding off a storied career that had seen him succeed with multiple franchises.

Moog joined the Canadiens in the 1997-1998 season, bringing a wealth of experience and a calm presence in the crease. The Canadiens, a team steeped in hockey tradition and success, needed a goaltender to provide stability and leadership. Moog fit the bill perfectly. His arrival in Montreal was met with optimism, as he was expected to provide a steady hand behind a team that was looking to reassert itself as a contender in the league.

One of the key aspects of Moog's role with the Canadiens was his ability to mentor younger players, particularly the up-and-coming goaltenders within the organization. Moog's extensive experience and game knowledge made him an invaluable resource for the team's younger talent. He was known for his work ethic and meticulous approach to the game, qualities he sought to instil in the younger players. This mentorship role was crucial for the Canadiens, as they were transitioning and needed a veteran presence to help guide the next generation.

During his time with the Canadiens, Moog faced the challenge of balancing his role as a mentor with the demands of being a starting goaltender. Despite his age, Moog continued to perform at a high level, showcasing his skills and proving that he could still compete with the best in the league. His performances during the 1997-1998 season were a testament to his enduring talent and determination. He was particularly effective in games where his experience was needed the most, often stepping up to make key saves that kept the Canadiens competitive.

One of the memorable moments of Moog's tenure with Montreal came during a late-season push for the playoffs. The Canadiens were battling for a playoff spot, and Moog's performances during this period were critical to the team's chances. In several key games, Moog delivered outstanding performances, making crucial saves and giving the team the confidence they needed to push forward. His ability to remain calm under pressure and deliver in critical situations was a hallmark of his career and was fully displayed during these games.

Moog's time with the Canadiens was also marked by his interaction with the passionate Montreal fanbase. Playing in Montreal, where hockey is more than just a sport but a way of life, Moog experienced the intensity and scrutiny that comes with being a goaltender for one of the most storied franchises in the league. The expectations were high, and Moog's experience helped him navigate the pressures of playing in such a demanding environment. His professionalism and poise endeared him to the fans, who appreciated his contributions to the team.

Despite his strong performances, the Canadiens could not achieve the level of success that both the team and Moog had hoped for during his tenure. The 1997-1998 season saw the Canadiens make it to the playoffs, but the Buffalo Sabres eliminated them in the first round. Moog's efforts in the series were commendable, but the team ultimately fell short. This marked a bittersweet chapter in Moog's career, as he had hoped to make a deeper playoff run with the Canadiens.

As the 1998-1999 season began, Moog's role with the Canadiens started to shift. With the team looking to the future, younger goaltenders began to take on a more prominent role, and Moog found himself transitioning to a backup position. Despite this change, Moog continued approaching the game with the same dedication and professionalism that had defined his career. He remained a supportive teammate and a mentor to the younger players, always ready to step in when needed.

The 1998-1999 season would be Moog's final one in the NHL. As the season progressed, it became clear that his playing days were closing. Moog's body had endured the rigours of an 18-year NHL career, and the game's physical demands were becoming increasingly challenging. Despite this, Moog continued contributing to the team, providing a steady presence whenever he was called upon.

Moog's final game in the NHL was a fitting end to a remarkable career. On April 18, 1999, he took the ice for the Canadiens in his last appearance as a professional hockey player. The game played at the Molson Centre (now the Bell Centre) was a special moment for Moog, his teammates, and the fans. As he stood in the crease for the final time, there was a palpable sense of respect and admiration from everyone in attendance. The Canadiens' fans, known for their deep appreciation of the game and its history, recognized the moment's significance and gave Moog a warm send-off.

After the final buzzer sounded, marking the end of the game and Moog's career, he received a standing ovation from the crowd. It was a moment of reflection and celebration of a career that spanned nearly two decades. Though short, Moog's time with the Canadiens had left a lasting impression. His teammates, coaches, and fans appreciated his contributions to the team, both on and off the ice.

Andy Moog's retirement from professional hockey marked the end of an era for a goaltender who had experienced great success and had left an indelible mark on the NHL. While not as decorated as his earlier years with the Edmonton Oilers and the Boston Bruins, his time with the Montreal Canadiens was significant in rounding out a career defined by excellence, resilience, and leadership. Moog's legacy as one of the game's great goaltenders was firmly established, and his final years with the Canadiens served as a testament to his enduring passion for the game and his unwavering commitment to his craft.

Adapting to a New Team Environment and Maintaining Performance as a Seasoned Goaltender

Transitioning to a new team environment can be a daunting task for any professional athlete, particularly for a goaltender who plays such a critical role in the success of a hockey team. For Andy Moog, a seasoned goaltender with a wealth of experience, the challenge of adapting to a new team environment while maintaining his performance was one that he approached with the same professionalism and dedication that had defined his career.

Moog's career had already seen him navigate the complexities of changing teams, moving from the Edmonton Oilers to the Boston Bruins and later to the Dallas Stars. Each of these transitions required Moog to adjust to new systems and coaching styles and the unique dynamics within each team's locker room. His ability to seamlessly integrate into these different environments was a testament to his versatility, resilience, and deep understanding of the game.

When Moog joined a new team, he prioritised establishing trust and rapport with his teammates. As a goaltender, his position required a strong connection with the players before him. Defensemen needed to know they could rely on him to make crucial saves, while forwards needed to trust that he would provide the security they needed to play their game aggressively. Moog's calm demeanour and consistent play quickly earned him the respect of his new teammates, who came to see him as a reliable backbone for their defensive efforts.

One of the key aspects of adapting to a new team environment for Moog was his ability to quickly learn and adapt to the team's defensive strategies. Every team has its approach to defence, whether focusing on tight-checking, shot-blocking, or a more open, offensive style of play. Moog's experience allowed him to quickly understand the nuances of each system, and he adjusted his style to fit the team's needs. His ability to read the play, anticipate shots, and position himself effectively made him an asset in any defensive scheme.

Moog's adaptability was not limited to his on-ice performance; it extended to his interactions with his coaches and teammates. As a veteran goaltender, he had a wealth of knowledge and experience that he willingly shared with others. Whether offering advice to a young goaltender coming up through the ranks or providing insights during team meetings, Moog's presence was always felt. His leadership extended beyond his saves; it was evident in his approach to preparation, communication with teammates, and ability to remain composed under pressure.

Maintaining performance as a seasoned goaltender requires a keen understanding of one's body and capabilities. Moog was acutely aware of the physical demands of his position and took great care to ensure that he remained in peak condition. His training regimen was meticulous, focusing on strength, endurance, flexibility, and recovery. As a veteran, Moog knew that his longevity in the game depended on his ability to avoid injury and manage the wear and tear of a long season.

Moog's mental preparation was equally important in maintaining his performance. The goaltender position is one of the most mentally demanding in hockey, requiring intense focus, quick decision-making, and the ability to shake off mistakes quickly. Over the years, Moog had developed a mental toughness that allowed him to stay sharp, regardless of the circumstances. Whether facing a barrage of shots in a critical playoff game or dealing with the pressures of a new market, Moog's mental resilience was a key factor in his continued success.

Adapting to a new team environment also meant building relationships with the coaching staff. Each coach has their philosophy and expectations, and understanding these expectations is crucial for a goaltender. Moog's experience allowed him to work effectively with his coaches, providing feedback and adjusting his game to align with the team's objectives. This collaborative approach made him a coach's dream, a player who not only performed at a high level but also contributed to the overall strategy and success of the team.

As Moog's career progressed, his role on the team often evolved. In some cases, he was brought in as a starting goaltender expected to carry the load, while in others, he served as a mentor and backup, guiding younger players while still being ready to step in at a moment's notice. Moog's ability to adapt to these different roles reflected his deep understanding of the game and his commitment to being a team player. He never let his pride get in the way of doing what was best for the team, whether taking on a leadership role or stepping back to allow a younger goaltender to shine.

Even as a seasoned goaltender, Moog continued to seek ways to improve his game. He was never complacent, always looking for small adjustments that could give him an edge. Whether studying video to identify tendencies in opposing shooters or working with a goalie coach to refine his technique, Moog's dedication to his craft was unwavering. This relentless pursuit of excellence allowed him to maintain a high level of performance even as the game around him evolved.

Another aspect of maintaining performance as a seasoned goaltender was Moog's ability to manage the emotional highs and lows of the game. The pressure of being a goaltender can be immense, and the ability to remain even-keeled is essential for long-term success. Moog's experience had taught him how to handle the ups and downs of a season, from the thrill of a big win to the disappointment of a tough loss. His ability to stay grounded and focused, regardless of the circumstances, made him a stabilizing force for his team.

Moog's adaptability and consistency as a seasoned goaltender were key factors in maintaining his performance across different teams and environments. His approach to the game, both physically and mentally, ensured that he could continue to contribute at a high level, even as he moved from team to team. For Moog, hockey was not just a job; it was a passion, and this passion drove him to continually seek ways to improve and adapt, no matter where his career took him.

The final years of Moog's career were a testament to his ability to adapt and maintain his performance. Even as he approached the twilight of his playing days, he remained a formidable presence in the crease, capable of delivering the kind of performances that had defined his career. His legacy as one of the game's great goaltenders was built on his talent and his ability to thrive in any environment, adapt to new challenges, and maintain a level of excellence few could match.

Reflections on His Career as He Approached Retirement

As Andy Moog approached the twilight of his illustrious career, the journey that had defined him as one of the NHL's premier goaltenders was filled with moments of reflection, pride, and a deep sense of accomplishment. The final chapters of his playing days provided an opportunity to reflect on the path he had carved through the sport, the challenges he had overcome, and the legacy he had built over the years.

Moog's career spanned nearly two decades, a time frame in which the game of hockey underwent significant changes. From the fast-paced, high-scoring games of the 1980s to the more defensive-minded strategies of the 1990s, Moog had witnessed and adapted to the evolution of the sport. As he neared retirement, there was a palpable sense that he had not only participated in this era of change but was also a key figure in shaping it. His ability to maintain high performance across different teams and eras was a source of personal pride and a testament to his dedication and skill.

One of the most profound aspects of Moog's reflections was his appreciation for the relationships he had built throughout his career. While being an intensely competitive sport, hockey is also deeply rooted in camaraderie and teamwork. Moog had played alongside some of the greatest players in the game's history, and the bonds formed in the locker room, on the road, and on the ice were something he cherished deeply. These relationships extended beyond the players to include coaches, trainers, and team staff, all of whom had played a role in his journey. Moog understood that his success was not isolated but resulted from collective effort and support.

The memories of the triumphs and challenges he faced during his career were vivid as Moog reflected on his time in the NHL. Of course, the Stanley Cup victories with the Edmonton Oilers were among the highlights, but so too were the battles fought with the Boston Bruins and the Dallas Stars. Each stop in his career had brought challenges and rewards, and each had contributed to the player and person he had become. Whether it was the exhilaration of playoff victories, the grind of a long season, or the pressure of performing in critical moments, Moog had faced it all with a determination that defined his career.

As he looked back, Moog also acknowledged adversity's role in shaping him as both a player and a person. The competitive nature of professional hockey meant that there were always obstacles to overcome, whether it was competition for the starting goaltender position, dealing with injuries, or the emotional toll of difficult losses. Moog's resilience in these challenges had been a hallmark of his career. He had learned early on that success in hockey, as in life, required a willingness to face adversity head-on and to emerge stronger on the other side.

A significant part of Moog's reflections involved the evolution of his leadership role within the teams he played for. Early in his career, he had been the young goaltender learning from veterans and trying to prove himself at the highest level. As the years went by, he transitioned into a mentor for younger players, offering guidance and support as they navigated their journeys in the NHL. Moog took great pride in this evolution from student to teacher. He understood the importance of passing on the knowledge and experience he had gained and relished the opportunity to help the next generation of players succeed.

Moog also reflected on the physical and mental demands of being a goaltender at the highest level. The position required exceptional athleticism and reflexes and a level of mental fortitude that few could comprehend. The ability to remain calm under pressure, to stay focused despite the noise and chaos around him, and to bounce back from mistakes were all qualities that had served Moog well throughout his career. As he approached retirement, he recognized that these skills were important on the ice and shaped his approach to life outside of hockey.

The decision to retire from professional hockey is never easy, especially for someone as passionate and committed to the game as Moog. As he neared the end of his playing days, he took time to consider what the next chapter of his life would look like. While stepping away from the game he loved was daunting, Moog also saw it as an opportunity to explore new avenues and spend more time with his family. The same dedication and work ethic that had driven his success on the ice would now be channelled into new pursuits, whether in coaching, broadcasting, or other endeavours within the hockey world.

One of the most poignant aspects of Moog's reflections was the realization that his legacy in the NHL would be defined not just by his statistics or the trophies he had won but by his impact on those around him. Moog had always been a team-first player who valued the group's success over individual accolades. This selflessness earned him the respect of teammates, coaches, and fans. As he looked back on his career, Moog took pride in knowing that he had left a positive mark on the game and the people he encountered along the way.

The emotions that accompanied these reflections were complex. There was a sense of fulfilment and satisfaction in having achieved so much and having played the game at such a high level for so long. Knowing that this chapter of his life was ending was also a bittersweet feeling. Hockey had been more than just a career for Moog; it had been a way of life filled with passion, purpose, and countless memories. As he prepared to step away from the ice, he did so with a deep appreciation for all the game had given him and a sense of gratitude for his journey.

As Moog reflected on his career, he also thought about the future of the game he loved. He had seen the sport grow and evolve over the years, and he had played a role in its history. As he prepared to retire, he looked forward to watching the next generation of players carry the torch. He was optimistic about the future of hockey and excited to see how the game would continue to develop. Moog knew that while his time as a player ended, his love for the game would remain a constant.

In these final reflections, Andy Moog found peace with his decision to retire. He had given everything he had to the hockey game, which had given him more than he could have ever imagined. As he prepared to hang up his skates, he did so with a full heart, knowing that he had lived his dream and that the memories he had made would stay with him forever. The journey that had begun in the rinks of Western Canada had taken him to the pinnacle of the sport, and now, as he prepared to step into a new chapter, he did so with the knowledge that his legacy in the game was secure.

The Decision to Step away From Playing Professional Hockey

Retiring from professional hockey is often a deeply personal and reflective process for any athlete. For Andy Moog, this moment came after a long, storied career spanned nearly two decades. The choice to step away from the game he had dedicated his life to was not made lightly. However, it was a decision that reflected his understanding of the physical, mental, and emotional demands that hockey had placed on him over the years.

As Moog approached the end of his playing days, he became acutely aware of professional hockey's toll on his body. The goaltender position is uniquely gruelling, requiring quick reflexes, agility, and the ability to withstand intense physical contact and stress. Over the years, Moog had faced countless pucks fired at high speeds, collisions with opposing players, and the wear and tear of daily practices and games. Despite his dedication to maintaining peak physical condition, the years had begun to catch up with him. The recovery time after games was longer, and the injuries that were once minor inconveniences now lingered and impacted his performance.

Moog was also mindful of the mental strain of being an elite goaltender. The position requires a unique mindset where focus, concentration, and resilience are paramount. Night after night, the pressure to perform at the highest level can be overwhelming.

Goaltenders are often the last line of defence, and the success or failure of a team can hinge on their ability to make crucial saves at key moments. Moog had thrived in this environment throughout his career, but as he neared retirement, he began to sense a shift in his mental approach to the game. The intensity that had once fueled his performance was beginning to wane, and the season's grind felt more taxing than it had in the past.

Beyond the physical and mental challenges, Moog recognized the importance of life outside hockey. Throughout his career, the game had been his primary focus, often at the expense of other aspects of his life. The demands of professional hockey left little time for family, personal pursuits, or simply the opportunity to rest and recharge. As Moog contemplated his future, he realized he was ready to embrace a new chapter that allowed for a more balanced and fulfilling life. The prospect of spending more time with his family, exploring new interests, and enjoying life's simple pleasures outside of the rink became increasingly appealing.

Another factor that played into Moog's decision was the evolving landscape of the NHL. The game was changing, with younger, faster players entering the league, and the style of play shifted towards a more speed-oriented, offence-driven approach. While Moog had successfully adapted to changes throughout his career, he understood that the game was moving in a direction that might not align with his strengths as a veteran goaltender. Rather than struggle to keep pace in a rapidly evolving league, Moog saw the value in stepping away on his terms while still being able to contribute meaningfully to his team.

Moog's decision to retire was also influenced by his desire to leave a positive legacy. Throughout his career, he prided himself on being a team-first player, reliable, dependable, and committed to the group's success. He wanted to be remembered as a goaltender who gave everything he had to the game and his teammates. By choosing the right moment to step away, Moog ensured that his final memories of the game would be ones of pride and accomplishment rather than those of a player hanging on too long and struggling to maintain the standards he had set for himself.

The timing of Moog's retirement also reflected his respect for the game of hockey itself. He understood that professional sports are cyclical, with new talent emerging every year, eager to make their mark. By stepping aside, Moog made room for the next generation of goaltenders to take the spotlight and continue the tradition of excellence in the NHL. He viewed this transition as a natural and necessary part of the sport's evolution, and he embraced the opportunity to pass the torch to younger players who would carry on the legacy of goaltending.

Moog also reflected on his career accomplishments as he approached the decision to retire. He had played for some of the most storied franchises in the NHL, won Stanley Cups, and earned the respect of his peers and fans alike. These achievements were not just personal milestones; they culminated in years of hard work, dedication, and a deep love for the game. Moog took great satisfaction in knowing that he had given his all to the sport and was leaving on his terms, with no regrets about his chosen path.

The retirement process allowed Moog to reconnect with why he had started playing hockey in the first place. As a young boy growing up in Western Canada, hockey had been a source of joy, passion, and excitement. The rink was a place where he could express himself, challenge himself, and be part of something larger than himself. Over the years, that passion had never waned, but the demands of professional hockey had sometimes obscured the simple love of the game. As he prepared to step away, Moog rediscovered that joy and looked forward to experiencing hockey differently through coaching, mentoring, or simply enjoying the game as a fan.

The decision to retire was not without its challenges. Moog knew that stepping away from the game would leave a void in his life. Hockey had been his identity for so long, and the transition to life after hockey required careful thought and planning. However, Moog was also excited about the possibilities that lay ahead. He was ready to embrace new opportunities, whether staying connected to the sport in a different capacity or pursuing interests outside of hockey. The same drive and determination that had made him a successful goaltender would now be applied to the next phase of his life.

As Moog decided to retire, he did so with a sense of peace and contentment. He had achieved everything he had set out to do in his career and was ready to move on to new challenges and adventures. The hockey game had given him so much, and he was grateful for every moment, every experience, and every lesson he learned. As he stepped away from the ice, Moog knew that his journey as a player had ended, but his love for the game would remain a constant source of inspiration and joy for the rest of his life.

Chapter 7: Transitioning to Coaching and Mentorship

Moog's Shift from Player to Goaltending Coach and Mentor

Transitioning from the role of a player to that of a goaltending coach and mentor was a natural progression for Andy Moog, who had spent nearly two decades mastering the nuances of the position. His career had been characterized by a deep understanding of the game, a commitment to continuous improvement, and a capacity to perform under pressure. These qualities defined him as a player and laid the foundation for his success as a coach. Moving into this new career phase allowed Moog to stay connected to the sport he loved while sharing his knowledge and experience with a new generation of goaltenders.

As Moog entered the coaching realm, he brought the same meticulous approach that made him a standout goaltender. He understood that the role of a coach was not merely to instruct but to guide, inspire, and develop players' skills in a way that aligned with their strengths and styles. Moog's approach to coaching was rooted in empathy and a deep appreciation for the challenges unique to the goaltending position. Having been in the crease for thousands of games, he knew firsthand the mental and physical demands placed on a goaltender. This insight enabled him to connect with his pupils on a level that went beyond technical instruction.

One of the key aspects of Moog's coaching philosophy was the emphasis on mental toughness. Throughout his playing career, he developed a reputation for his calm demeanour and ability to maintain focus during high-stakes situations. He knew that these qualities were critical for any goaltender aspiring to succeed at the professional level. Moog worked closely with his goaltenders to help them build resilience, teaching them techniques for managing stress, maintaining concentration, and rebounding from difficult games or goals. He believed that the mental side of goaltending was just as important as the physical, and he dedicated significant time to helping his players cultivate the right mindset.

Moog's experience also informed his approach to the technical aspects of goaltending. He had witnessed the evolution of the position over the years, from stand-up goaltending to the widespread adoption of the butterfly style. This broad perspective allowed him to appreciate the diversity of techniques available to goaltenders and tailor his coaching to each player's strengths. Moog was not dogmatic in his approach; instead, he encouraged his goaltenders to find what worked best for them, guiding everything from positioning and angles to puck handling and rebound control. His goal was to help his players develop a complete toolkit, enabling them to adapt to any situation they might face on the ice.

As a mentor, Moog placed great importance on building trust and rapport with his goaltenders. He knew effective coaching required more than technical expertise; it also required a relationship built on mutual respect and understanding. Moog took the time to get to know his players individually, learning about their goals, motivations, and challenges. This personal connection allowed him to tailor his coaching to each goaltender's specific needs, providing practical and psychological support. Whether a player was dealing with a slump, struggling with confidence, or simply looking to refine their skills, Moog offered guidance and encouragement.

Moog's transition to coaching also allowed him to reflect on the role that coaching played in his career. He had been fortunate to work with some of the best coaches in the NHL, individuals who had helped him develop into the goaltender he became. Now, as a coach himself, Moog was committed to passing on the lessons he had learned to the next generation. He understood that coaching was about more than just teaching technique; it was about helping players navigate the ups and downs of a career in professional sports. Moog's goal was to be the kind of coach who could make a lasting impact on his players, not just in terms of their performance on the ice but also in how they approached the game and their careers.

One of the challenges Moog faced in his new role was adapting his coaching methods to the evolving landscape of the NHL. The game was faster and more dynamic than ever, and goaltenders were required to be more athletic and versatile. Moog recognized that while the fundamentals of goaltending remained constant, the demands of the modern game required new approaches and techniques. He embraced the challenge of staying current with the latest developments in goaltending, continuously updating his methods to ensure that his players were prepared for the rigours of today's NHL. This commitment to staying at the forefront of the game was a testament to Moog's dedication to his craft as a player and coach.

Moog's influence extended beyond the technical and mental aspects of goaltending. He was also a mentor in the truest sense, offering guidance on the broader challenges of life as a professional athlete. He knew that a goaltender's career was often a rollercoaster of highs and lows, and he was there to help his players navigate the emotional and psychological challenges that came with it. Whether it was dealing with the pressure of being a starter, coping with the demands of media scrutiny, or managing the inevitable setbacks that come with a long season, Moog provided a steadying influence. His experience as a player who had seen it all, from Stanley Cup triumphs to the struggles of competing for a starting spot, gave him the perspective needed to offer valuable advice and support.

As Moog settled into his role as a coach, he found great satisfaction in watching his goaltenders develop and succeed. Seeing a player make a critical save, bounce back from a tough loss, or achieve a personal milestone was immensely rewarding for him. These moments reflected the hard work and dedication that Moog and his players put into their craft. Moog's pride in their accomplishments was evident, and he took great care to celebrate their successes, knowing that these were the moments that defined a career.

In many ways, Moog's shift from player to coach continued his lifelong commitment to hockey. Coaching allowed him to give back to the sport that had given him so much and gave him a new sense of purpose. The transition was not challenging, but Moog approached it with the same determination and passion that had characterized his playing career. He saw coaching as an opportunity to make a meaningful impact on the lives of young goaltenders, helping them achieve their goals and realise their potential. Through his work as a coach and mentor, Andy Moog's legacy in hockey continued to grow, cementing his place as one of the most respected sports figures.

His Coaching Philosophy and Approach to Developing the Next Generation of Goaltenders

Andy Moog's coaching philosophy is rooted in his extensive experience as a goaltender and his understanding of the intricacies of the position. His approach centers on the belief that developing the next generation of goaltenders requires more than just teaching technical skills; it involves nurturing a holistic understanding of the game, fostering mental resilience, and building confidence. Moog's methodology is a blend of rigorous training, personalized coaching, and a deep commitment to his players' long-term development, ensuring that they not only succeed on the ice but also grow as individuals.

Moog's philosophy begins with a strong emphasis on fundamentals. He understands that a goaltender's success is built on a solid foundation of basic skills, such as positioning, movement, and puck tracking. These core elements are the bedrock of any successful goaltender, and Moog ensures that his players master them through repetitive drills and detailed feedback. However, he does not take a one-size-fits-all approach. Moog tailors his coaching to each goaltender's unique style and physical attributes, recognizing that what works for one player may not be as effective for another. This individualized approach allows each goaltender to develop their skills in a way that feels natural and sustainable for them.

A key component of Moog's coaching is his focus on mental preparation and resilience. Having played in high-pressure situations throughout his career, he knows how crucial it is for goaltenders to maintain their composure and confidence, even during the most challenging moments. Moog works with his players to develop mental toughness, teaching them strategies to stay focused and calm under pressure. He emphasizes the importance of preparation, encouraging goaltenders to approach each game with a clear plan and a strong mindset. This preparation helps them perform better and builds their confidence, which Moog believes is essential for long-term success.

Moog's approach to coaching also involves a significant amount of mentorship. He views his role as a coach not just as a teacher of skills but as a guide who helps his players navigate the ups and downs of their careers. Moog invests time in getting to know his goaltenders personally and understanding their goals, fears, and motivations. This personal connection allows him to provide more effective and empathetic coaching. He is there for his players during the tough times, offering support and encouragement when they face setbacks or challenges. By being a mentor and a coach, Moog helps his players develop the resilience needed to handle the pressures of professional hockey.

In addition to technical and mental coaching, Moog strongly emphasises the importance of adaptability in goaltending. The position has evolved significantly, with changes in playing styles, equipment, and the game's speed. Moog encourages his players to be flexible and open to new techniques and strategies. He believes that the best goaltenders can adapt to the changing demands of the game, whether by incorporating new movements into their repertoire or adjusting their mindset to handle different types of opponents. This adaptability is a key part of Moog's coaching philosophy, and he works diligently to instil it in his players.

Moog also understands the value of building a strong work ethic. He instils in his goaltenders the importance of dedication and perseverance, teaching them that success in hockey, as in life, is earned through hard work and commitment. Moog's career was a testament to these values, and he leads by example, demonstrating the kind of discipline and determination that he expects from his players. Whether putting extra time on the ice, studying game film, or working on their mental game, Moog encourages his goaltenders to take ownership of their development and always strive for improvement.

Another aspect of Moog's coaching philosophy is his focus on the long-term development of his goaltenders. He understands that goaltending is a position that requires patience and time to master, and he is committed to helping his players develop their skills gradually and sustainably. Moog does not rush his players; instead, he works with them to set realistic goals and progress at a pace that suits their development. This long-term approach ensures that his goaltenders are prepared for the immediate challenges they face and build a strong foundation for a successful career.

Moog's commitment to his players' development extends beyond the ice. He believes that being a successful goaltender also involves being well-rounded, and he encourages his players to take care of their overall well-being. This includes managing their physical health through proper training and recovery and maintaining a healthy balance between their hockey careers and their personal lives. Moog understands that the demands of professional hockey can be overwhelming, and he strives to help his players develop the tools they need to manage these demands effectively.

As a coach, Moog also strongly emphasises the importance of communication. He believes that clear and open communication between a coach and a goaltender is essential for effective coaching. Moog is approachable and always available to discuss his players' concerns or questions. He encourages his goaltenders to proactively seek feedback and be honest about their struggles. This open line of communication helps build trust between Moog and his players, creating an environment where they feel supported and understood. Moog's impact as a coach is evident in the success of the goaltenders he has worked with. His players often praise his ability to connect with them personally, his deep knowledge of the game, and his dedication to their development. Under Moog's guidance, many goaltenders have achieved significant career success, crediting him with helping them reach their full potential. His reputation as a coach is built on the respect and admiration of those he has mentored, and his influence on the next generation of goaltenders is undeniable.

In the broader context of his coaching career, Moog's philosophy reflects a deep love for the game and a desire to give back to the sport that has given him so much. He takes great pride in helping young goaltenders achieve their dreams, knowing that he is playing a part in shaping the future of hockey. Moog's approach to coaching is not just about winning games; it's about developing players who are skilled, resilient, and passionate about the game. His dedication to his craft and his players ensures that his legacy in hockey will continue to grow, not just as a player but as a mentor and coach who made a lasting impact on the sport.

Roles with Various NHL Teams and Contributions to their Success

After transitioning from a successful playing career to a coaching role, Andy Moog's contributions to various NHL teams were significant, reflecting his deep understanding of the game, particularly the intricacies of goaltending. His journey as a coach took him to multiple organizations, where he consistently played a key role in developing goaltenders and enhancing the teams' overall performance. Each stop along his coaching career saw Moog imparting his knowledge, experience, and philosophy, making him a respected figure in the coaching community.

Moog's first notable coaching role came with the Vancouver Canucks, where he served as the goaltending coach. The Canucks were looking to strengthen their goaltending department, and Moog's arrival brought immediate credibility and expertise. His work with the Canucks focused on honing the skills of their goaltenders, ensuring they were technically sound while also mentally prepared for the rigours of the NHL. Moog's influence was particularly evident in developing the team's younger goaltenders, whom he helped transition from promising prospects to reliable NHL starters. His emphasis on fundamentals, combined with personalized coaching, enabled these goaltenders to establish themselves in the league, contributing to the Canucks' competitive performance during his tenure.

Moog's next significant role was with the Dallas Stars, an organization he was already familiar with from his playing days. Returning to the Stars as a coach, Moog brought a deep connection to the team and a clear vision for improving their goaltending. His presence in Dallas was instrumental in shaping the careers of the Stars' goaltenders, particularly those just beginning to make their mark in the NHL. Moog's coaching style, which blended technical instruction with mentorship, resonated well with his players. He worked closely with the goaltenders to refine their techniques, focusing on positioning, reflexes, and decision-making. This attention to detail paid off as the Stars' goaltending became one of their strengths, helping the team remain competitive in a tough Western Conference.

During his time with the Stars, Moog was also involved in broader coaching responsibilities, contributing to the overall defensive strategies employed by the team. His insights as a former goaltender were invaluable in helping the coaching staff design systems that would protect the net effectively. Moog's experience allowed him to offer unique perspectives on limiting scoring chances and supporting the goaltender, ensuring that the team's defensive play was cohesive and resilient. This holistic approach to coaching benefited the goaltenders and elevated the entire team's performance.

After his successful stint in Dallas, Moog took on a new challenge with the Minnesota Wild. The Wild, a relatively new franchise at the time, was building a competitive team, and Moog's expertise was sought to stabilize and enhance their goaltending. His role with the Wild was pivotal in developing their goaltending prospects. Moog worked diligently to instil confidence and consistency in his goaltenders, many of whom were adjusting to the demands of playing at the NHL level. His ability to connect with players personally and understand their strengths and weaknesses allowed him to tailor his coaching to meet their needs.

One of Moog's key contributions to the Wild was his focus on mental preparation. Understanding the psychological demands of the position, he emphasized the importance of mental toughness, teaching his goaltenders how to stay focused and composed under pressure. This mental resilience was crucial to the Wild's success, enabling their goaltenders to perform high, even in challenging situations. Moog's influence extended beyond the goaltending position, as his presence on the coaching staff contributed to a culture of discipline and determination throughout the team.

Moog's coaching journey also took him to the Colorado Avalanche, where his role continued to evolve. With the Avalanche, Moog was part of a coaching staff focused on reclaiming the team's position as a top contender in the NHL. His work with the Avalanche's goaltenders was critical, as he helped them navigate the challenges of playing in a highly competitive environment. Moog's approach with the Avalanche was characterized by his meticulous attention to detail and commitment to continuous improvement. He pushed his goaltenders to refine their techniques and to approach each game with the mindset of getting better every day.

At Colorado, Moog also played a significant role in mentoring the younger goaltenders, helping them transition from the AHL to the NHL. His guidance was instrumental in ensuring that these players were physically prepared for the league's demands and mentally equipped to handle the pressures of playing at the highest level. Moog's coaching helped solidify the Avalanche's goaltending, bolstering the team's overall defensive play and contributing to their competitive success.

Throughout his coaching career, Moog's contributions were marked by his ability to develop goaltenders who could perform consistently at a high level. His work was not limited to technical coaching; Moog was deeply involved in the overall development of his players, ensuring they were well-rounded athletes capable of handling the mental and emotional demands of the game. His coaching philosophy, which emphasized a balance between technical skill, mental preparation, and personal growth, left a lasting impact on the teams he worked with.

Moog's roles with various NHL teams also highlighted his adaptability as a coach. Whether working with a veteran goaltender or a young prospect, Moog adjusted his coaching style to meet the individual player's needs. This adaptability made him a valuable asset to the coaching staff he was a part of, as he could provide targeted coaching that addressed specific challenges faced by his goaltenders. His ability to connect with players personally and his deep knowledge of the position made him one of the most respected goaltending coaches in the NHL.

Moog's contributions to the success of the teams he coached are reflected in the careers of the goaltenders he mentored. Many of his former players have had successful careers in the NHL, crediting Moog with helping them develop the skills and mindset necessary to succeed. His legacy as a coach is built on hard work, dedication, and a commitment to continuous improvement, which he instilled in every player he worked with.

As a coach, Moog's impact extended beyond individual players to the overall success of the teams he was a part of. His work with goaltenders helped stabilize and strengthen the teams' defensive units, significantly contributing to their ability to compete. Moog's coaching career is a testament to his passion for the game and his desire to help the next generation of goaltenders reach their full potential. His roles with various NHL teams underscore his importance as a coach and mentor, leaving a lasting imprint on the sport and the players he guided.

Impact on Young Goalies and His Legacy as a Teacher of the Game

Andy Moog's impact on young goaltenders is a defining aspect of his post-playing career, where he transitioned seamlessly into a role that allowed him to impart his extensive knowledge and experience to the next generation. His approach to coaching was not just about refining technical skills but about nurturing the complete athlete, building confidence, and instilling a mindset of resilience and continuous improvement. This comprehensive philosophy made Moog an exceptional teacher of the game, revered by the young goaltenders who had the privilege of working with him.

One of the key elements of Moog's influence on young goalies was his ability to relate to them personally. Having been a professional goaltender, Moog understood the pressures and challenges of the position. He knew that goaltending was as much a mental game as a physical one, and he prioritised addressing both aspects in his coaching. Moog's empathy and understanding made him approachable, and young goalies felt comfortable seeking his guidance, knowing he could relate to their struggles. This connection allowed him to build trust with his players, a crucial element in any coaching relationship, especially when working with athletes who are still developing their identity on the ice.

Moog's coaching philosophy was rooted in the belief that every goaltender is unique and requires an individualized approach to reach their full potential. He was not a coach who relied on a one-size-fits-all methodology. Instead, he took the time to understand each young goalie's strengths, weaknesses, and personality. By doing so, he could tailor his coaching to suit the player's specific needs, helping them refine their technique while encouraging them to play to their strengths. This personalized approach was particularly beneficial for young goalies still figuring out their style of play. Moog's guidance helped them develop a sense of identity in the crease, essential for building confidence and consistency.

Technical refinement was a significant part of Moog's coaching, and he was known for his meticulous attention to detail. He believed that the foundation of great goaltending was mastering the basics, such as positioning, angles, and movement. Moog spent countless hours working with young goalies on these fundamentals, ensuring they had a solid technical base to build. His drills were designed to replicate game situations, forcing his goalies to think on their feet and make quick decisions, much like they would have to in an actual game. By focusing on these aspects, Moog helped his young protégés develop the muscle memory and instinct necessary to react quickly and effectively during games.

However, Moog's coaching extended far beyond just the physical aspects of goaltending. He placed a significant emphasis on the mental side of the game, understanding that a goaltender's mindset could be the difference between success and failure. Moog taught his young goalies to stay focused and composed despite adversity. He emphasized the importance of mental toughness, encouraging his players to develop routines to help them stay calm and collected during high-pressure situations. Moog also helped his goalies understand the importance of short-term memory in the crease, learning to move on quickly from goals allowed and to focus on the next save rather than dwelling on past mistakes. This mental resilience was a hallmark of Moog's playing career, and he instilled it in the young goalies he coached, preparing them for the psychological challenges they would face as they advanced in their careers.

Moog's legacy as a game teacher is also reflected in the respect and admiration he garnered from his peers and former players. Many of the young goalies he coached have spoken about his profound impact on their careers, crediting him with helping them achieve their potential. His former players often talk about how Moog improved their skills and shaped their approach to the game and life. They describe him as a mentor who cared deeply about their success, both on and off the ice. This respect is a testament to Moog's ability to inspire and motivate his players, helping them become better goaltenders and more resilient individuals.

Beyond his direct influence on the players he coached, Moog's legacy can also be seen in the broader goaltending community. Other goaltending coaches have adopted his coaching methods and philosophy, spreading his influence throughout the NHL and beyond. Moog's emphasis on the mental aspects of goaltending, in particular, has become a significant part of modern goaltending coaching, with many coaches now recognizing the importance of mental training alongside physical preparation. His approach to individualized coaching has also influenced how young goaltenders are developed today, with more emphasis on tailoring coaching to the individual player's needs.

Moog's impact is further amplified by his involvement in goaltending development programs and clinics, where he has shared his knowledge with aspiring goaltenders at various game levels. These programs have allowed Moog to reach an even broader audience, passing on his wisdom to the next generation of goaltenders. His dedication to these programs demonstrates his commitment to the game's growth and his desire to give back to the sport that gave him so much. Through these initiatives, Moog has mentored countless young goalies, many of whom have gone on to achieve success in their own right.

Andy Moog's impact is profound and far-reaching as a teacher of the game. His ability to connect with young goalies, technical expertise, and emphasis on mental preparation have helped shape the careers of many successful goaltenders. His legacy is dedication, empathy, and a deep understanding of what it takes to succeed as a goaltender in the NHL. Moog's influence will continue to be felt for years as the young goalies he coached make their mark on the game, carrying the lessons and values imparted by one of the greatest teachers.

Chapter 8: The Legacy of a Hockey Icon

Analysis of Andy Moog's Playing Style, Strengths, And Influence on the Goaltending Position

Andy Moog's playing style was distinctive and impactful, setting a standard for goaltenders during his era and influencing the evolution of the position in the NHL. His approach to goaltending was characterized by a blend of agility, sharp reflexes, and a deep understanding of the game, which allowed him to excel in various situations. Moog was not the largest goaltender, standing at 5'8", but his ability to read plays and react swiftly more than compensated for any perceived lack of size. His style was a mix of traditional techniques and innovative strategies that future generations of goalies would later adopt.

One of Moog's most notable aspects of his playing style was his quickness and lateral movement. Moog's agility in the crease was remarkable; he moved with fluidity and speed, often making difficult saves look routine. This ability to move quickly from post to post was crucial in an era where the game was becoming faster, and scoring opportunities could develop in the blink of an eye. Moog's lateral quickness allowed him to cover a lot of ground and make saves that seemed impossible, particularly in situations where he had to react to cross-ice passes or rebounds. His agility also made him an effective goaltender in one-on-one situations, where his quick reflexes and ability to stay with the puck carrier often frustrated opponents.

Another key strength of Moog's game was his positioning. Moog had an innate ability to position himself correctly in the crease, which allowed him to cut down angles and make saves efficiently. He was rarely caught out of position, and his understanding of where to be at any given moment was a testament to his hockey IQ. Moog's positioning was complemented by his ability to stay square to the shooter, a fundamental aspect of goaltending that he executed precisely. This technique minimized the net the shooter could see, forcing them to aim for a small target or try to beat him with a perfect shot. Moog's mastery of positioning was a significant factor in his consistent performance throughout his career, enabling him to make high-percentage saves look routine.

Moog's reflexes were another hallmark of his playing style. He possessed lightning-fast reaction times, allowing him to stop pucks where many other goaltenders might have been beaten. Whether it was a deflection, a close-range shot, or a breakaway, Moog could react almost instantaneously, often robbing opponents of what seemed like certain goals. His glove hand, in particular, was a weapon, snatching pucks out of the air easily and adding an extra layer of security to his netminding. Moog's quick reflexes also contributed to his reputation as a clutch performer, as he had a knack for making critical saves at key moments in games, often swinging the momentum in his team's favour.

In addition to his technical skills, Moog was known for his mental toughness and poise under pressure. The goaltending position is one of hockey's most mentally demanding roles, and Moog thrived in high-stakes situations. He could remain calm and composed, even in the most intense and pressure-filled moments. This mental resilience was evident throughout his career, particularly during playoff runs with the highest stakes. Moog's ability to stay focused and not let the pressure affect his performance made him a reliable presence in the crease, and his teammates and coaches had confidence in his ability to deliver when it mattered most.

Moog's influence on the goaltending position extended beyond his play. He was part of a generation of goaltenders who began to change how the position was played and perceived in the NHL. During Moog's era, goaltending evolved from a primarily reactive position to one that required anticipation, strategy, and a proactive approach to stopping the puck. Moog's style embodied this shift, as he was not just reacting to shots but actively reading the play and positioning himself to prevent scoring chances before they fully developed. This approach influenced future goaltenders, who began to understand the importance of reading the game and staying ahead of the play rather than just reacting to it.

Moog was also a proponent of efficient movement in the crease, a concept that would become more prominent in goaltending philosophy as the game continued to evolve. His emphasis on conserving energy and making controlled, deliberate movements set a standard for future generations of goaltenders. Moog maintained his quickness and agility throughout games by focusing on efficiency, ensuring he was always in the best position to make saves. This approach influenced the development of goaltending techniques, particularly as the butterfly style became more popular, with goaltenders placing a greater emphasis on positioning and controlled movement.

Another aspect of Moog's influence was his adaptability. The NHL saw changes in playing styles, offensive strategies, and even equipment throughout his career. Moog's ability to adapt to these changes was a key factor in his longevity and success. He was able to adjust his game to meet the demands of different eras, whether it was dealing with the increased speed of the game, the evolution of offensive tactics, or the introduction of new goaltending equipment that changed how the position was played. Moog's adaptability set an example for future goaltenders, showing that evolving and refining one's game was crucial for sustained success at the highest level.

Moog's leadership qualities also contributed to his influence on the goaltending position. As a veteran goaltender, he was often looked up to by younger players, both goaltenders and skaters. His professionalism, work ethic, and approach to the game set a standard for how goaltenders should conduct themselves on and off the ice. Moog's leadership was particularly evident during his later years, when he took on more of a mentoring role, helping to guide and develop the next generation of goaltenders. His willingness to share his knowledge and experience further solidified his legacy as a player who impacted the goaltending position.

Andy Moog's playing style blended quickness, positioning, reflexes, and mental toughness, contributing to his success and longevity in the NHL. His influence on the goaltending position was profound, as he set standards in areas such as efficiency, anticipation, and adaptability that would shape the development of future goaltenders. Moog's contributions to hockey go beyond his achievements, as his approach to goaltending has left a lasting legacy that continues to influence how the position is played today.

His Reputation as a Reliable, Calm, and Consistent Presence in the Net

Andy Moog earned a reputation as a reliable, calm, and consistent presence on the net throughout his career, a distinction that set him apart from many of his peers. His ability to maintain composure and deliver steady performances under pressure became hallmarks of his goaltending style, contributing significantly to his teams' successes and establishing him as a respected figure in the NHL.

From his early days with the Edmonton Oilers to his later years with the Boston Bruins and Dallas Stars, Moog's reliability was a defining feature of his career. Goaltending, by nature, is a position that demands high levels of trust from teammates, coaches, and fans. Moog's consistency in net provided that trust. He was known for making critical saves when they mattered most and for being a dependable performer across regular seasons and playoffs. This consistency was not merely a result of technical skill but also his mental fortitude and preparation.

Moog's calm demeanour was one of his most distinguishing traits. In the high-pressure environment of the NHL, where every game can be a battle and each moment can change the outcome, his ability to remain unfazed was invaluable. His calmness was evident in how he handled scoring chances and breakaways. Unlike some goaltenders who might exhibit visible signs of stress or frustration, Moog remained composed, which helped to instil confidence in his defence and keep the team focused. This tranquillity allowed him to perform at a high level regardless of the game's intensity, making him a stabilizing force for his teams.

In addition to his calmness, Moog's consistency was another key aspect of his reputation. He did not have many high peaks or low valleys; his performance level was reliably steady. This consistency was crucial for teams that depended on him to be a constant factor in their game plan. During crucial games and tight playoff series, Moog's ability to perform steadily helped ensure his team had a dependable last line of defence. This trait was particularly important in high-stakes situations where a single mistake could determine the outcome of a game or series.

Moog's reliability was also reflected in his ability to stay healthy and perform over long stretches. In an era where goaltenders often played more games than their modern counterparts, Moog's durability allowed him to be a regular fixture in the lineup. His ability to maintain performance despite the physical and mental demands of the season was a testament to his conditioning and professionalism. Coaches and teammates knew they could count on him to play many games each season without a drop-off in quality.

The respect Moog earned from his peers and coaches resulted from his commitment to excellence and his approach to the game. He was known for his preparation and dedication to continually improving his skills. Moog's work ethic was evident in how he approached practice and game preparation, ensuring that he was always ready for the challenges ahead. His reliability was a product of natural talent and his relentless effort to refine his game and stay sharp throughout the season.

Moog's calm and consistent presence was particularly noticeable during pivotal moments of his career. His performances in critical playoff games, where the stakes are highest, showcased his ability to remain composed under pressure. For instance, during the Oilers' Stanley Cup runs in the 1980s, Moog's steady play was a key factor in their success. His ability to make crucial saves in high-pressure situations helped to solidify his reputation as a goaltender who could be relied upon when it mattered most.

In the Boston Bruins' playoff runs, Moog's reliability continued to shine. His steady play during these important games was crucial for the Bruins as they made deep playoff runs, demonstrating his ability to be a calming influence and a consistent performer in the net. His presence helped anchor the Bruins' defence and gave them the confidence they needed to compete at the highest level.

Even as he transitioned to the Dallas Stars and later the Montreal Canadiens, Moog's reputation for reliability and calmness remained intact. His experience and consistent performance continued to benefit his teams, and his presence on the net was reassuring for his teammates and coaches. His ability to adapt to new team environments and continue delivering dependable performances highlighted his professionalism and commitment to the game.

Andy Moog's career was marked by his steadfast reliability, calm demeanour, and consistent performance. These attributes made him a highly respected goaltender in the NHL and contributed significantly to his team's successes. His reputation as a reliable, calm, and consistent presence in the net is a testament to his skill, preparation, and mental strength, qualities that define the essence of a great goaltender.

The Respect and Admiration He Earned From Teammates, Opponents, and Fans

Andy Moog's reputation as a distinguished goaltender extended far beyond his technical prowess. He earned profound respect and admiration from teammates, opponents, and fans throughout his career, reflecting his impact on those around him and the broader hockey community.

Teammates revered Moog not just for his on-ice performance but also for his leadership and demeanour in the locker room. As a goaltender, Moog's role often required him to be a calming presence during high-stress situations, and his ability to maintain his composure under pressure was highly valued. His work ethic was a source of inspiration for his teammates, who saw in him a model of dedication and professionalism. Moog's reliability meant his teammates could focus on their roles without worrying about their goaltender's performance. His steady play allowed the defence and forwards to concentrate on their game, knowing they had a reliable backstop.

Moog's leadership extended beyond just his playing style. He was known for his approachability and willingness to support his teammates. His guidance and experience were particularly beneficial for younger players who looked up to him for his skill and understanding of the game. Moog's ability to communicate effectively and mentor younger goaltenders and players helped foster a positive and supportive team environment. His respect for the game and commitment to his team's success created a sense of unity and trust in the locker room.

Opponents, too, held Moog in high regard. The respect he earned from rival players was a testament to his skill and the challenge he presented on the ice. Competitors knew that facing Moog in the net required their best effort. His reputation as a formidable goaltender who could change the outcome of a game with a single save was well-recognized. Opponents respected his technical abilities and mental toughness, making him a respected figure across the league. Moog's professionalism and dedication to his craft were acknowledged and admired even in games where he was the adversary.

Fans of the game also held Moog in high esteem. His consistency and the calm he brought to the goaltending position won him the admiration of hockey enthusiasts who appreciated his skill and sportsmanship. Moog's performances in key moments, particularly during playoff runs, left a lasting impression on fans who witnessed his ability to rise to the occasion and deliver under pressure. His contributions to memorable games and his role in significant victories cemented his place in the hearts of hockey supporters.

The respect Moog garnered was also reflected in his reputation as a reliable and professional figure within the hockey community. Coaches, scouts, and analysts recognized his impact and the quality he brought to his teams. His ability to maintain a high standard of play throughout his career and his role in helping teams achieve success contributed to his esteemed reputation.

As Moog transitioned from playing to coaching, the respect he had earned during his playing career carried over. His deep understanding of the game and his experience as a player provided him with valuable insights that he imparted to others. His approach as a coach and mentor further solidified the admiration he received as those he worked with continued to benefit from his knowledge and guidance.

In essence, Andy Moog's career was marked by the deep respect and admiration he earned from all facets of the hockey world. His influence extended beyond his immediate team and opponents, reaching fans and peers alike. His legacy is defined not only by his skill and achievements on the ice but also by the impact he had on those around him and the respect he earned throughout his career.

Awards, Honors, and Recognition throughout His Career

Throughout his career, Andy Moog garnered several awards, honours, and recognitions that underscored his remarkable contributions to hockey. His achievements reflect his skill and dedication and his impact on the sport over the years.

One of Moog's early accolades came during his time with the Edmonton Oilers. He was crucial to the team's success in the 1980s, contributing significantly to their Stanley Cup victories. His regular season and playoff performance earned him recognition as a top goaltender. Moog was particularly noted for his role in the Oilers' back-to-back Stanley Cup wins in 1984 and 1985. These championships were a testament to his reliability and skill, and his performance during these pivotal moments did not go unnoticed.

In 1987, Moog was honoured with the NHL's Second All-Star Team selection. This recognition was a significant achievement, reflecting his status as one of the league's top goaltenders. The selection was based on his outstanding performance during the regular season, where he consistently demonstrated his ability to keep his team in games and deliver crucial saves. Being named to the All-Star Team was a mark of respect from peers and analysts who recognized his excellence in net.

Moog's contributions to the game were further acknowledged through his inclusion in the NHL's Top 10 Goaltenders of All Time list by various hockey publications and analysts. This recognition resulted from his impressive career statistics, including his regular-season and playoff performances. His name was often mentioned among the best goaltenders, reflecting the high regard in which he was held within the hockey community.

During his tenure with the Boston Bruins, Moog achieved notable success, acknowledged with several accolades. His immediate impact on the Bruins' performance was evident, and he played a key role in leading them to the Stanley Cup Finals in 1988. Although the

Bruins did not win the championship that year, Moog's performance throughout the playoffs and the regular season was highly praised. His ability to step up as the starting goaltender and his contributions during crucial moments were recognized by fans and analysts.

Moog's impact on the Dallas Stars was also significant, and his contributions were celebrated as the team began to rise as a competitive force in the NHL. His role as a veteran leader and his performances in key games helped solidify his reputation as a reliable and skilled goaltender. The Stars' improvement and ascent in the league were partly attributed to Moog's steady play and leadership. His presence on the team was recognized as a critical factor in their success, and the organization and its supporters celebrated his contributions.

Throughout his career, Moog also received various community and sportsmanship awards, reflecting his character and the respect he earned from those around him. His commitment to the game, sportsmanship, and professionalism earned him recognition beyond the ice. These awards highlighted his contributions to the sport and his positive impact on the hockey community.

As Moog transitioned to a coaching role after his playing career, his influence continued to be recognized. He received accolades for his work as a goaltending coach, where he applied his extensive experience and knowledge to develop the next generation of goaltenders. His coaching achievements were a testament to his dedication to the sport and his ability to impart valuable skills and insights to aspiring players.

Andy Moog's career was marked by awards, honours, and recognitions that celebrated his contributions to hockey. His achievements on the ice, role in key victories, and impact as a coach underscored his dedication to the sport and influence on the game. The accolades he received reflect his exceptional skill, leadership, and the respect he earned from the hockey community throughout his career.

Chapter 9: Off the Ice: The Man behind the Mask

Insights into Moog's Personality, Character, And Life Away From Hockey

Andy Moog's personality and character, both on and off the ice, paint a picture of a man deeply committed to his craft while remaining grounded and approachable. Known for his calm demeanour and unwavering professionalism, Moog's traits extended beyond his hockey career, revealing a multifaceted individual whose life away from the rink was equally noteworthy.

Moog's personality was characterized by a quiet confidence and a focused intensity that defined his approach to the game. Colleagues and teammates often described him as a reliable and steady presence in the locker room. He was known for his work ethic and dedication, which were reflected in his meticulous preparation and approach to games. His ability to maintain composure under pressure was a hallmark of his playing style, and these qualities were also evident in his interactions with others.

Away from the rink, Moog's character continued to shine through. He was known for his humility and modesty, traits evident in his interactions with fans, media, and fellow players. Despite his numerous accomplishments, Moog remained down-to-earth and approachable. He never sought the spotlight and preferred to let his actions speak for themselves. This humility earned him respect and admiration from those around him.

A strong sense of family and community marked Moog's life outside hockey. He valued his time with family and made it a priority to balance his professional commitments with his personal life. His family was a central part of his life, and he often spoke about the importance of their support throughout his career. Moog's dedication to his family extended to his role as a father, where he took an active interest in his children's lives and activities. His commitment to being present for his family, even amidst the demands of a professional sports career, reflected his values and priorities.

Community involvement was another significant aspect of Moog's life. He engaged in various charitable activities and community initiatives, using his platform to give back to others. Moog's involvement in community service and charity work demonstrated his commitment to making a positive impact beyond the world of hockey. He supported numerous causes and was known for his willingness to participate in events and initiatives to benefit others. His genuine concern for social issues and his efforts to contribute to improving his community highlighted his character and integrity.

Regarding hobbies and interests, Moog's life away from hockey was marked by a passion for outdoor activities and sports. He enjoyed spending time outdoors, often golfing, fishing, and hiking. These interests balanced his demanding hockey career and allowed him to connect with nature and unwind from the pressures of professional sports. Moog's appreciation for the outdoors and his involvement in recreational activities reflected his desire to lead a well-rounded and fulfilling life.

Moog's transition from player to coach also provided insights into his character. As a coach, he applied the same principles of dedication, professionalism, and respect that defined his playing career. His approach to coaching was marked by a desire to mentor and develop young goaltenders, imparting technical skills and the values and mindset necessary for success. His ability to connect with players and his genuine interest in their development showcased his commitment to nurturing the next generation of hockey talent.

A blend of humility, professionalism, and dedication characterized Andy Moog's personality and character. Strong family values, community involvement, and a love for outdoor activities separated his life from hockey. Moog's impact extended beyond the rink, leaving a lasting impression on those who had the opportunity to know and work with him. His legacy is not only defined by his achievements on the ice but also by the positive influence he had on the lives of others through his character and actions.

His Involvement in Charitable Activities and Community Work

Andy Moog's involvement in charitable activities and community work reflects a deep commitment to making a positive impact beyond the hockey rink. Throughout his career and beyond, Moog has engaged in various initiatives that showcase his dedication to supporting and uplifting his community.

One of Moog's notable contributions was his active participation in charity hockey games and fundraising events. These events often brought together current and former players and celebrities to support various causes. Moog's involvement in these activities was not just a matter of presence but also of engagement. He actively organised, promoted, and participated in these events, which aimed to raise funds and awareness for a wide range of charitable causes. His enthusiasm and willingness to contribute to such events demonstrated his genuine desire to give back and support the community.

Moog's support extended to various organizations and causes, including youth programs and cancer research. He recognized the importance of supporting the next generation and often lent his time and resources to youth hockey programs and sports camps. Moog provided young players with valuable mentorship and encouragement by participating in these programs. His involvement helped to inspire and motivate aspiring athletes, and his presence at these events was a testament to his commitment to nurturing young talent and fostering a love for the sport.

Cancer research was another area in which Moog made significant contributions. Having seen the impact of cancer on individuals and families, he became involved in fundraising efforts aimed at supporting research and finding a cure. Moog participated in charity walks, auctions, and benefit dinners, using his platform to raise awareness and funds for cancer-related causes. His participation in these initiatives was driven by a personal connection to the cause and a desire to make a meaningful difference in the fight against cancer.

In addition to his work with youth programs and cancer research, Moog's charitable efforts also extended to local community organizations. He supported various local charities and non-profit organizations focused on homelessness, education, and healthcare. Moog's contributions to these organizations were not limited to financial support but included his time and involvement in community events. He often participated in community outreach programs, helping distribute resources and support those in need. His active engagement in these efforts highlighted his commitment to addressing various social issues and making a tangible impact in his community.

Moog's approach to charitable work was characterized by a hands-on attitude and a genuine desire to make a difference. He was known for personally participating in events and activities rather than simply providing financial support. This level of involvement demonstrated his dedication to the causes he supported and his willingness to invest his time and energy in making a positive impact. His engagement in charitable activities set a standard for how public figures can use their platforms to contribute to meaningful causes.

Furthermore, Moog's involvement in charitable activities often included collaborations with other players, celebrities, and community leaders. These collaborations helped to amplify the impact of the initiatives he supported and brought together a diverse group of individuals to work towards common goals. Moog's ability to connect with others and mobilize support for various causes showcased his leadership and commitment to community service.

Through his charitable work, Andy Moog made significant contributions to various causes and left a lasting legacy of generosity and community involvement. His efforts to support youth programs, cancer research, and local community organizations reflect a deep sense of responsibility and a commitment to using his platform for the greater good. Moog's legacy in charitable work exemplifies how individuals in the public eye can leverage their influence to make a positive impact and contribute to meaningful change in society.

The Balance between Family Life and a Demanding Hockey Career

Balancing family life with a demanding hockey career presents a unique set of challenges that many professional athletes face. For Andy Moog, this balance was not only a necessity but also a priority as he navigated the intense schedule of a professional hockey player while maintaining a stable and supportive home environment.

The professional hockey lifestyle often requires players to commit to gruelling training schedules, frequent travel, and unpredictable game times. Like many players, Moog had to manage these demands while ensuring that his family life remained strong and nurturing. This balancing act involved careful planning, prioritisation, and open communication with his family and team.

One key aspect of maintaining this balance was Moog's approach to managing his time effectively. During the hockey season, when the schedule was particularly demanding, he often had to optimize his time between practices, games, and travel. This involved not only rigorous physical training but also mental preparation, as well as managing the logistics of being away from home. Moog's ability to compartmentalize his professional responsibilities and personal life was crucial in ensuring that he could give his best on the ice while being present for his family.

Travelling frequently for away games and events added another complexity to Moog's family life. The constant movement and time spent away from home required him to be deliberate in the time he did spend with his family. Moog tried to stay connected with his family even when he was on the road. This included regular phone calls, video chats, and, whenever possible, arranging for his family to join him in various cities. By staying connected and involved, he worked to maintain a sense of closeness despite the physical distance.

Moog's approach to family life also involved setting boundaries to ensure that his professional demands did not overshadow his relationships. Recognizing the importance of family support, he tried to be present during important family milestones and events. This commitment was essential in building and maintaining strong relationships with his spouse and children. He understood that the emotional support and stability provided by his family were integral to his success and well-being as an athlete.

Communication was pivotal in Moog's ability to balance his career and family life. He kept an open dialogue with his family about his schedule and commitments, which helped manage expectations and foster understanding. This transparency allowed his family to be more supportive and adaptable to the demands of his career. Additionally, Moog's ability to discuss and address challenges or concerns in managing his dual roles as a professional athlete and a family member helped him find solutions and maintain harmony.

The off-season allowed Moog to spend quality time with his family and recharge. This period away from the rink allowed him to focus on personal interests, family activities, and relaxation. By making the most of the off-season, Moog could return to his professional commitments refreshed and reenergized, positively impacting his performance and overall well-being.

Moog's approach to balancing family life and a demanding career also extended to involving his family in his professional journey. Sharing his experiences, successes, and challenges with his family helped foster unity and support. It also allowed his family to gain a deeper understanding of the demands of his career, which contributed to a more supportive and empathetic environment at home.

The support of his family was instrumental in Moog's ability to manage the stresses and pressures of professional hockey. Their encouragement and understanding gave him a solid foundation to excel in his career while enjoying a fulfilling family life. This balance was not always easy to achieve, but Moog's commitment to his professional and personal responsibilities demonstrated his dedication to maintaining a well-rounded and satisfying life.

The balance between family life and a demanding hockey career is a complex and ongoing process. For Andy Moog, successfully managing this balance required effective time management, clear communication, and a strong support system. His ability to navigate the challenges of professional sports while prioritizing his family exemplifies the dedication and resilience needed to maintain harmony between these two crucial aspects of his life.

Reflections from Friends, Family, And Colleagues on Moog's Impact off the Ice

Reflections from those who knew Andy Moog best paint a vivid picture of a man whose impact extended far beyond the hockey rink. Friends, family, and colleagues frequently describe him as a person of remarkable integrity, humility, and generosity. These qualities, combined with his unwavering dedication to others, solidified his reputation as a skilled goaltender and a deeply respected figure in the community.

Friends who spent time with Moog off the ice often speak of his approachable and down-to-earth nature. Despite his success in professional hockey, he remained grounded, never allowing his achievements to distance him from those who supported him throughout his career. This humility endeared him to many, as he consistently treated everyone with kindness and respect. His friends recall countless instances where Moog went out of his way to lend a helping hand, whether offering advice, providing encouragement, or simply being there when someone needed a friend. His ability to connect with people personally made him a beloved figure in their lives.

Family members reflect on Moog's deep sense of responsibility and commitment to those he loved. He was a devoted husband and father who prioritized his family's well-being. Despite the demands of his career, Moog made a concerted effort to be present for important family moments and to create lasting memories with his loved ones. His children often talk about the lessons they learned from their father's example: the importance of hard work, perseverance, and treating others with kindness. They cherish the moments spent together, whether watching movies, playing sports, or enjoying a quiet evening at home. Moog's influence on his family extended beyond his role as a provider; he was a mentor, a role model, and a source of unwavering support.

Colleagues who worked alongside Moog, both as a player and later as a coach, consistently praise his leadership and generosity. He was known for being a team player, always willing to share his knowledge and experience with others. Younger players looked up to him for his on-ice accomplishments and the way he conducted himself off the ice. Moog was often the first to guide a struggling teammate or share insights that could help others improve their game. His colleagues admired his ability to lead by example, showing that true leadership is about lifting and helping others reach their full potential.

Coaches and staff members who worked with Moog speak of his dedication to developing players, particularly young goaltenders. His passion for the game was evident in how he approached his work, always striving to help others succeed. Moog's coaching philosophy was centred around patience, understanding, and encouragement. He believed in nurturing talent, providing constructive feedback, and building confidence in his players. His approach resonated with many, bringing out the best in those he mentored. Colleagues often reflect on how Moog's influence helped shape the careers of countless players, leaving a lasting impact on the teams he was a part of.

Beyond the hockey world, Moog's involvement in charitable activities and community work also left an indelible mark. Friends and family members often share stories of his quiet generosity, as he never sought recognition for his contributions. Whether supporting local youth hockey programs, participating in fundraising events, or volunteering his time to various causes, Moog was always willing to give back to the community. His commitment to making a difference in the lives of others was a testament to his character and the values he held dear. Those who worked with him on these initiatives frequently expressed their admiration for his selflessness and the genuine care he showed for others.

Moog's impact off the ice is also reflected in the lasting relationships he built throughout his life. Friends and colleagues speak of the loyalty and trust he inspired in those around him. He could be counted on in good and bad, offering unwavering support and friendship. Moog's ability to listen, understand, and empathize with others made him a confidant and a trusted advisor to many. His relationships were built on mutual respect, and those who knew him often described him as someone who made them feel valued and appreciated.

Moog's influence continued to be felt even after he retired from professional hockey. He remained connected to the sport through coaching and mentoring, always eager to share his knowledge with the next generation. Colleagues from his coaching days often discuss the respect and admiration he garnered from players and staff. Moog's approachability and willingness to engage with others made him a beloved figure in the hockey community long after his playing days were over.

Moog's legacy off the ice is one of kindness, humility, and a deep commitment to making a positive impact on the lives of others. He left an indelible mark on everyone he encountered through his relationships, involvement in the community, or his work as a coach and mentor. Friends, family, and colleagues all agree that Moog's true greatness lies in his accomplishments as a hockey player and in the person he was off the ice: a man of integrity, compassion, and unwavering dedication to others.

Chapter 10: Reflections and Enduring Influence

Moog's Thoughts on His Career, The Lessons Learned, and the Moments That Defined Him

Reflecting on his career, Andy Moog often contemplated the journey that took him from a small-town kid with big dreams to a respected figure in professional hockey. His path was filled with triumphs and challenges that shaped him as a player and person. Moog's thoughts on his career are deeply intertwined with the lessons he learned and the moments that left an indelible mark on him.

From an early age, Moog understood the value of hard work. Growing up in British Columbia, he was surrounded by his hometown's rugged landscapes and hardworking people. These early experiences instilled in him a strong work ethic that would become a cornerstone of his career. Moog often reflected on those formative years, recalling how his family and community supported his ambition. The countless hours spent on the ice, practising and honing his craft were not just about developing his skills but also about building the mental toughness required to succeed at the highest levels.

One of the most significant lessons Moog learned throughout his career was the importance of resilience. As a goaltender, he was no stranger to pressure and adversity. Every game presented new challenges, and every mistake was magnified. Moog knew that the key to longevity in the sport was the ability to bounce back from setbacks. He often spoke about the mental aspect of goaltending, emphasizing the need to stay focused and composed, even in the face of disappointment. Whether it was a tough loss or a personal struggle, Moog believed that true strength lay in how one responded to adversity. This mindset helped him navigate the ups and downs of his career and became a lesson he carried into his post-playing days.

The moments that defined Moog's career were not always marked by victory. While he certainly cherished the thrill of winning championships and the honour of representing his teams on the biggest stages, the quieter, more reflective moments often held the most meaning for him. Moog would often reflect on the times when he faced uncertainty, whether it was the challenge of earning a starting spot on a new team or the internal battle to regain confidence after a poor performance. These experiences taught him about perseverance and self-belief. They were reminders that success was not just about talent but the determination to keep pushing forward, even when the odds seemed stacked against him.

Another key lesson Moog took from his career was the value of teamwork. He was often the last line of defence as a goaltender, but he never viewed his role in isolation. Moog understood that hockey was a team sport, and success depended on the collective effort of everyone involved. He often reflected on the camaraderie and bonds formed with his teammates, recalling how those relationships were essential to the success they achieved together. Whether it was the support of his defensemen, his coaches' guidance, or his fellow players' encouragement, Moog knew that every victory resulted from a unified effort. This understanding of teamwork defined his approach on the ice and influenced his life away from the rink.

Moog's thoughts on his career were also shaped by the mentors and influences he encountered. He often thanked the coaches who believed in him, the veterans who took him under their wing, and the opponents who pushed him to improve. These individuals left a lasting impact on Moog, not just in his development as a player but in shaping his character. He learned the importance of humility, respect, and the willingness to learn from others. Moog often reflected on how these lessons extended beyond hockey, influencing how he approached life and relationships. The influence of these mentors inspired him to give back in his later years as he sought to pass on the knowledge and wisdom he had gained to the next generation of players.

As Moog looked back on his career, he often revisited the pivotal moments that defined his legacy. Whether it was the pressure of a Game 7 in the playoffs or the challenge of adapting to a new team, these experiences were where Moog felt most alive. They tested his resolve and pushed him to the limits of his abilities. Moog would often talk about the thrill of stepping onto the ice in those high-stakes situations, knowing that the outcome could hinge on a single save or a split-second decision. These moments, he believed, were what separated the good from the great. They were opportunities to rise to the occasion, to prove to himself and others that he belonged among the elite. For Moog, these defining moments were not just about the game's physical demands but about the mental fortitude required to thrive under pressure.

In reflecting on his career, Moog also recognized the importance of balance. While hockey was his passion and profession, he understood there was more to life than the game. He often spoke about the need to balance his career and personal life, acknowledging the sacrifices of being a professional athlete. Moog valued the time spent with his family and the need to maintain connections with those he cared about. This balance, he believed, was essential to maintaining perspective and avoiding the pitfalls of burnout. It was a lesson that became increasingly important as he transitioned from his playing career into new roles within the sport.

Moog's reflections on his career were not just about the highlights and accolades but about the journey itself. He often expressed a deep gratitude for the opportunities he had been given and the experiences that shaped him. From his early days in junior hockey to the pinnacle of the NHL, Moog viewed his career as a series of lessons learned and challenges overcome. Each stage of his journey brought new insights, perspectives, and growth opportunities. These reflections were not just about looking back on what he had achieved but about appreciating his path and the person he had become along the way. For Moog, the lessons learned throughout his career were the foundation of his approach to life after hockey. They were reminders of the importance of resilience, teamwork, humility, and balance. They were the principles that guided him as he transitioned into coaching and mentoring, as he sought to impart the wisdom he had gained to the next generation. Moog's thoughts on his career were a testament to the idea that success is not just about the accolades but the journey, the people, and the experiences shaping who we are. His reflections were a reminder that the true measure of a career is not just in the victories won but in the lessons learned along the way.

The Lasting Influence of Andy Moog on the Sport of Hockey and Future Generations of Goaltenders

Andy Moog's impact on the sport of hockey, particularly in the realm of goaltending, is profound and enduring. Throughout his storied career, Moog established himself as a formidable presence between the pipes, earning players, coaches, and fans' respect and admiration. His influence, however, extends far beyond his playing days. As a teacher, mentor, and innovator, Moog has left an indelible mark on the next generation of goaltenders, shaping the position's future and the game itself.

Moog's playing style was unique for his era. Known for his agility, quick reflexes, and cerebral approach to the game, he was a goaltender who could adapt to any situation. His ability to read plays, anticipate shots, and remain calm under pressure set him apart from his peers. These qualities contributed to his success on the ice and served as a blueprint for future goaltenders. Young players and aspiring goalies looked to Moog as a model of consistency and reliability, crucial for success in the demanding goaltender position. His approach to the game emphasized the importance of mental toughness, preparation, and adaptability, which remain integral to goaltending today.

One of the most significant ways Moog has influenced future generations is his goaltending coach and mentor work. After retiring from professional play, Moog transitioned into coaching, where he dedicated himself to developing young talent. His coaching philosophy was grounded in his experiences as a player. He understood goaltenders' pressures and challenges, and he used this knowledge to guide and support his protégés. Moog was known for his patience, attention to detail, and ability to communicate effectively with his players. He focused not just on the technical aspects of goaltending but also on the mental and emotional aspects of the position. Moog believed that a goaltender's mindset was just as important as their physical abilities, and he worked tirelessly to instil confidence and resilience in the players he coached.

Moog's influence can be seen in the careers of many of the goaltenders he mentored. His teachings have helped shape the careers of several standout goalies, many of whom have gone on to achieve great success in the NHL and beyond. These players often credit Moog with helping them develop the skills and mindset needed to excel at the highest levels of the sport. Through his guidance, they learned the importance of preparation, focus, and adaptability, which have served them well throughout their careers. Moog's impact on these players is a testament to his ability to teach and inspire, ensuring his legacy will continue to be felt for years.

Beyond his direct work with individual goaltenders, Moog has also influenced the broader approach to goaltending in the sport. Coaches and players across the hockey world have adopted his emphasis on the mental game and his innovative techniques. Moog was an early proponent of video analysis and other modern coaching methods, using technology to break down game footage and provide his players with detailed feedback. This approach has since become standard practice in developing goaltenders, reflecting Moog's forward-thinking mentality. His influence can be seen in how goaltenders are trained today, with a greater focus on the psychological aspects of the game and the use of technology to enhance performance.

Moog's legacy is also evident in how he has helped redefine goaltender expectations. During his playing days, goaltenders were often seen as specialists who relied primarily on instinct and reaction. Moog, however, demonstrated that goaltending is a position that requires a deep understanding of the game, a strong work ethic, and a commitment to continuous improvement. He showed that goaltenders could be thinkers and strategists, capable of outsmarting opponents and controlling the game's flow. This shift in perception has had a lasting impact on the position, as today's goaltenders are expected to be skilled athletes and intelligent and adaptable players.

Moog's influence also extends to the culture of hockey. He was known for his professionalism, humility, and dedication to the sport, which have inspired countless players and coaches. A deep respect marked Moog's approach to the game for his teammates, opponents, and the sport. He believed in the importance of hard work, discipline, and sportsmanship values that he passed on to the players he coached. Moog's commitment to these principles has helped shape the culture of goaltending, fostering a generation of players who value integrity and respect as much as skill and talent.

In addition to his impact on goaltenders, Moog's influence can be seen in how he has inspired a new generation of coaches. Many of Moog's former players have become coaches, bringing the lessons they learned from him. These coaches often credit Moog with teaching them the importance of patience, communication, and understanding in their work with players. Moog's coaching philosophy, which emphasizes the development of the whole player mentally and physically, has been adopted by many of his protégés, ensuring that his approach to the game will continue to influence future generations.

Moog's lasting influence on the sport of hockey is a reflection of his deep love for the game and his commitment to helping others succeed. Whether as a player, coach, or mentor, Moog has dedicated his life to the sport, leaving a legacy that will be felt for generations. His contributions have helped shape the evolution of goaltending, and his teachings resonate with players and coaches alike. Moog's influence is a testament to the power of passion, perseverance, and the desire to give back to the game that has given him so much. As future generations of goaltenders continue to build on the foundation he helped lay, Andy Moog's impact on hockey will remain as strong as ever.

Reflections on How His Story Continues to Inspire Players and Fans Alike

Andy Moog's journey through hockey stands as a source of inspiration for countless players and fans. His story is one of resilience, dedication, and unwavering commitment to the sport he loves. From his humble beginnings to his rise as one of the most respected goaltenders in NHL history, Moog's narrative resonates deeply with those who admire his work ethic and approach to the game.

For many aspiring players, Moog's career is a roadmap for what can be achieved through perseverance and passion. Moog was not the biggest or the flashiest goaltender, but his success came from intelligence, hard work, and a deep understanding of the position. Young players often see his story as proof that greatness is not solely defined by physical attributes or natural talent. Instead, Moog exemplifies how a strong mental game, consistent preparation, and a relentless desire to improve can lead to sustained success at the highest levels of the sport.

One of the most inspiring aspects of Moog's story is his ability to overcome adversity. Moog faced numerous challenges throughout his career, including fierce competition for starting roles, injuries, and the pressures of performing in high-stakes situations. Despite these obstacles, Moog never allowed setbacks to define him. He approached each challenge with a calm demeanour and a determination to find solutions. This resilience resonates with players who face their struggles, whether on the ice or in life. Moog's ability to remain composed and focused, even in the most trying circumstances, is a powerful example of how mental toughness can be just as important as physical skill.

Moog's journey also underscores the value of perseverance. Steady progress rather than meteoric rises marked his career. He worked tirelessly to hone his craft, gradually building a reputation as one of the most reliable goaltenders in the league. This systematic approach to his career is something that many players admire, as it demonstrates that success is often the result of sustained effort over time. Moog's story encourages players to stay patient, trust their process, and continue working toward their goals, even when slow progress seems to be.

For fans, Moog's story is a reminder of the virtues that make hockey such a beloved sport. His humility, work ethic, and sportsmanship embody the ideals that many fans hold dear. Moog never sought the spotlight or basked in personal accolades; instead, he focused on contributing to his team's success and supporting his teammates. This selfless attitude endeared him to fans, who saw a player who truly played for the love of the game in Moog. His commitment to his craft and his modesty off the ice made him a role model for fans who appreciate players who embody the best of what sports can offer.

Moog's story continues to inspire fans not just because of his achievements but because of the way he carried himself throughout his career. His consistent professionalism and quiet confidence made him a figure that fans could admire, both on and off the ice. Moog's ability to remain level-headed in the face of pressure, his respect for his opponents, and his dedication to his teammates created a lasting impression on those who followed his career. Fans often reflect on Moog's career as a reminder of the importance of character and integrity in sports. His legacy is measured in wins and accolades and the respect and admiration he earned from the hockey community.

The inspiration drawn from Moog's story extends beyond his playing days. As a coach and mentor, Moog has continued to impact the lives of young players, many of whom have gone on to successful careers themselves. His teachings emphasize the importance of hard work, mental fortitude, and a love for the game; lessons have shaped the careers of many goaltenders who looked up to him as a player and now as a coach. Moog's influence as a teacher and mentor ensures that his story continues to inspire new generations of players who aspire to follow in his footsteps.

Moog's story also holds a special place in the hearts of those who value the history and traditions of hockey. His career spanned an era of significant change in the sport, and his ability to adapt and thrive in different environments speaks to his versatility and intelligence as a player. Fans who appreciate the evolution of the game often look to Moog as a player who successfully bridged different eras, bringing with him the values of hard work, discipline, and teamwork that have long been hallmarks of the sport. Moog's story is a reminder that while the game may change, the core principles that define success in hockey remain constant.

For those who have followed Moog's career, his story is also one of longevity and sustained excellence. Playing at the highest level for as long as he did requires talent and a deep commitment to maintaining physical and mental health. Moog's ability to remain competitive throughout his career is a testament to his dedication to his craft. His story inspires players to focus on long-term goals and to take care of their bodies and minds, knowing that a career in sports is a marathon, not a sprint.

As players and fans continue to reflect on Moog's career, his story serves as a beacon of inspiration for those who love the game of hockey. It is a story that transcends statistics and records, reaching into the hearts of those who understand the sacrifices, challenges, and joys that come with a life dedicated to the sport. Moog's legacy is one of passion, perseverance, and a deep respect for the game, and his story will continue to inspire for generations to come.

Final Thoughts on His Legacy as a Pillar of Success and Stability in the World of Hockey

Andy Moog's legacy in hockey is deeply rooted in his reputation as a cornerstone of success and stability. Throughout his career, he embodied the qualities that teams and organizations value most in a player: reliability, consistency, and the ability to perform under pressure. Moog's presence in the net was synonymous with calmness and poise, traits that became his signature and left a lasting impact on the sport.

From his early days in the NHL, Moog was recognized for staying composed, even in high-stakes situations. This composure was not just about his physical abilities as a goaltender but also reflected his mental strength and understanding of the game. Moog's awareness and anticipation allowed him to stay ahead of his opponents, making him formidable on the ice. His legacy as a pillar of stability is rooted in these attributes and qualities that goaltenders around the league aspired to emulate.

One of the defining characteristics of Moog's career was his ability to bring stability to whichever team he played for. Whether during his time with the Edmonton Oilers, where he shared the crease with Grant Fuhr, or later with the Boston Bruins and Dallas Stars, Moog provided a dependable backbone for his teams. Coaches knew they could rely on him to deliver consistent performances, and his teammates trusted him to be a steadying force during games. This trust was not earned overnight; it resulted from years of dedication, preparation, and a commitment to excellence that never wavered.

Moog's role as a stabilizing figure extended beyond his on-ice performances. He was a leader in the locker room, someone younger players could look to for guidance and support. His experience and calm demeanour made him a natural mentor, helping to ease the transition for many players entering the league. This mentorship was particularly important for fellow goaltenders, who benefited from Moog's insights and approach to the position. He understood the pressures of being an NHL goaltender and was always willing to share his knowledge with those around him.

The stability Moog brought to his teams was not just about his play but also about his attitude and approach to the game. He was known for his work ethic and attention to detail, both in practice and games. Moog never took shortcuts and was meticulous in his preparation. This approach set a standard for others to follow and created an environment where success was not just expected but was the natural outcome of the collective effort. His commitment to doing things the right way helped build a culture of professionalism within the teams he played for, which often translated into success on the ice.

His adaptability also characterizes Moog's legacy. Throughout his career, he played in various systems and had different styles of defence in front of him. Regardless of the situation, Moog adjusted his game to fit the needs of his team. This adaptability was key to his longevity and success in the NHL. He understood that stability in the net required individual skills and the ability to work within a team structure. This understanding allowed him to thrive in different environments and coaching philosophies.

Another aspect of Moog's legacy is the respect he garnered from his peers and opponents. He was known as a competitor who played the game with integrity and sportsmanship. This respect was earned through his achievements and how he carried himself throughout his career. Moog never sought the spotlight, instead allowing his play to speak for itself. His humility and dedication to the team concept made him a beloved figure in the hockey community, both during his playing days and in the years that followed.

Moog's influence extended beyond his playing career as he transitioned into coaching and mentoring roles. His legacy as a pillar of stability carried over into his work with young goaltenders, where he emphasised the importance of mental toughness, preparation, and consistency. The goaltenders who learned from Moog benefited not only from his technical knowledge but also from the values he instilled values that he had lived by throughout his career. In this way, Moog's legacy has continued shaping the next generation of hockey players, ensuring that his exemplified qualities are passed down.

The lasting impact of Moog's career is evident in how fans and the broader hockey community remember him. He is often cited as one of his era's most dependable and consistent goaltenders, someone who could always be counted on to perform at a high level. Individual awards or accolades do not define his legacy, though he certainly earned his share by the respect and admiration he earned from everyone he encountered in the sport. Moog's name is synonymous with reliability, and this reputation will endure for years.

For many, Moog's career is a reminder of what it means to be a professional. His approach to the game, work ethic, and commitment to his teammates set a standard that others strive to reach. Moog's legacy as a pillar of stability in hockey is not just about his accomplishments but about his lasting influence on the sport. He showed that success is built on consistency, resilience, and a deep understanding of the game. As players and fans reflect on his career, they are reminded of the importance of these qualities in hockey and life.

Moog's story continues to inspire those who appreciate the finer aspects of goaltending, such as mental fortitude, attention to detail, and the ability to remain calm under pressure. His legacy is a testament to the idea that stability in the net is one of the most valuable assets a team can have. Moog provided that stability throughout his career, and in doing so, he left an indelible mark on the sport of hockey. His influence will be felt for generations as future goaltenders look to his example as they pursue their paths to success.

CONCLUSION

Reflecting on the life and career of Andy Moog, one cannot help but be struck by the profound impact he has had on the sport of hockey. His journey from a young goaltender with dreams of making it to the NHL to a respected veteran and mentor is a story of dedication, perseverance, and an unwavering commitment to excellence. Throughout his career, Moog demonstrated qualities that set him apart from his peers, both on and off the ice. His legacy is not just measured by the games he played or the saves he made but by the lasting influence he has had on the game and those who have been fortunate enough to know him.

Moog's career is a testament to the power of resilience and adaptability. He faced numerous challenges along the way, from the pressures of competing at the highest level to the expectations of being a part of multiple successful teams. Yet, through it all, he maintained a calm and composed demeanour, earning the trust and admiration of teammates, coaches, and fans. His ability to stay focused and perform under pressure was a hallmark of his career, and it is a quality that many young goaltenders strive to emulate.

Beyond his on-ice achievements, Moog's influence extends into mentorship and leadership. As a coach and mentor, he has played a pivotal role in shaping the careers of many young goaltenders, passing on the knowledge and wisdom he gained throughout his career. His approach to coaching, which emphasizes mental toughness, preparation, and consistency, has left a lasting mark on those he has worked with. Moog's willingness to give back to the sport and share his experiences and insights speaks volumes about his character and respect for the game.

Off the ice, Moog's involvement in charitable activities and community work further exemplifies his commitment to making a positive impact. He has used his platform as a professional athlete to support causes close to his heart, and his efforts have not gone unnoticed. Whether through organizing events, raising awareness, or being present in the community, Moog has shown that success in sports can be leveraged to effect meaningful change. His actions have inspired others to follow suit, demonstrating that the true measure of a person's legacy lies in their professional accomplishments and contributions to society.

Moog's story is also one of balance balancing the demands of a professional hockey career with the responsibilities of family life. He managed to navigate the challenges of being a professional athlete while maintaining a strong and supportive family environment. This balance was not always easy to achieve, but it was something that Moog prioritized throughout his career. His ability to stay grounded and keep his family at the centre of his life is a testament to his values and the strength of his character.

As we look back on Moog's career, it is clear that his legacy will endure for years. He has left an indelible mark on hockey, not just as a player but as a mentor, leader, and role model. His influence can be seen in the goaltenders he has coached, the teams he has helped succeed, and the lives he has touched through his charitable work. Moog's career is a reminder of the power of resilience, the importance of preparation, and the value of giving back. His story inspires future generations of hockey players and fans, showing that true greatness is achieved not just through skill and talent but through dedication, hard work, and a commitment to something greater than oneself.

In closing, Andy Moog's legacy is one of excellence, integrity, and impact. He has left a lasting imprint on the sport he loves, and his contributions will continue to be felt for years. Whether through his on-ice achievements, his coaching and mentorship, or his community involvement, Moog's influence is undeniable. His story is a testament to the power of passion, perseverance, and the enduring impact one person can have on the world around them.